A GUIDE TO
GOOD
BUSINESS
COMMUNICATION

A GUIDE TO
GOOD
BUSINESS
COMMUNICATION

5TH EDITION

HOW TO WRITE AND SPEAK ENGLISH
WELL IN EVERY BUSINESS SITUATION

MICHAEL BENNIE

howtobooks

Published by How To Books Ltd
Spring Hill House, Spring Hill Road,
Begbroke, Oxford OX5 1RX, United Kingdom
Tel: (01865) 375794. Fax: (01865) 379162
info@howtobooks.co.uk
www.howtobooks.co.uk

How To Books greatly reduce the carbon footprint of their books by sourcing
and printing in the UK.

Fifth edition 2009

British Library Cataloguing in Publication Data
A catalogue record for this book is available from the British Library

ISBN 978 1 84528 292 9

Produced for How to Books by Deer Park Productions, Tavistock
Typeset by Pantek Arts Ltd, Maidstone, Kent
Printed and bound by Bell and Bain Ltd, Glasgow

Contents

Introduction

Communication is the key to success in any business. Whether you are trying to sell a product, answer a query or complaint or convince your colleagues to adopt a certain course of action, good communication often means the difference between success and failure. At best, imprecise language, clumsy sentences or long-winded 'waffle', whether in speech or writing, will give a poor impression of you or your business; at worst, what you are trying to say will be misunderstood or ignored. In contrast, clear, precise English will be enjoyable to read or listen to, and is likely to evoke the response you want.

This book is written for everyone who wants to develop the skill of good communication in the workplace – from business students to managers, voluntary workers to government officials. Moreover, because of the globalisation of trade and the use of the Internet, the position of English as the international language of business is stronger than ever. I hope, therefore, that those who do not have English as their first language but need to use it for business communication will also find this a useful guide.

The aim is to give you a good grounding in writing and speaking style, which you can then apply to any situation. It shows what is good and bad style, what you should avoid and why. What it does not do is provide a set of model documents for particular situations. You should think about what you want to say, not just copy someone else's models. So although you will find a great many examples of documents throughout the book, they are just that – examples to illustrate particular points and techniques, not models to be copied.

The book is arranged in such a way as to be easy to use, whether you are following it from start to finish or dipping into it. It starts with a general discussion of business communication and then goes on to planning, layout, construction and style. There are chapters on grammar, punctuation and spelling, but I have put them towards the end. This is not because they are unimportant – far from it – but so that you can refer to them if you need to without them getting in the way of the discussion of style and construction. They contain the minimum of theory; the emphasis is on practical application, and on mistakes to avoid.

Throughout the book there are exercises in which you can put the techniques discussed into practice. Answers are provided at the back. In many cases (for example, when an exercise involves writing a letter or memo) there will be several possible options, depending on your own personal style, and the samples shown are just suggestions. In other instances, especially when it comes to grammar or spelling, there will clearly be only one answer, and in these cases that is made clear.

As you improve your communication skills, you will find it very satisfying to be able to express yourself clearly and succinctly, and to get your *precise* meaning across to your audience. Not only will you have the satisfaction of a job well done, but you will know that there is a greater chance that people will react in the way you want them to.

All the characters and organisations in the examples and exercises are purely fictional, and any resemblance to real individuals or organisations is purely coincidental.

CHAPTER 1
Communicating in business

Communication

The definition of communication is: The process by which information is exchanged. It can take place in a number of ways:

- through the written word
- through the spoken word
- through pictures and diagrams
- through facial expressions, behaviour and posture
- through non-verbal sounds

In business the most common forms of communication are spoken and written, although visual forms can play a part, as we shall see in Chapter 3.

The Functions of Business Communication

We communicate in business for a number of different reasons, and the methods we use will depend on the reasons, the circumstances, and perhaps the people with whom we are communicating. These are some of the reasons why we may need to communicate with others in a business setting:

- to pass on information
- to persuade people to buy a product or use a service
- to discuss an issue
- to recommend a course of action
- to make or answer a request
- to make or answer a complaint
- to keep a record of something that has happened or been agreed
- to explain or clarify a situation
- to give an instruction

Clearly, to cover such a variety of situations, you will need to be able to use a range of different methods and styles. Your style and tone are unlikely to be the same if you are making a request, for example, as if you are making a complaint. You are also more likely to speak to someone than to write to them if you want to discuss an issue, whereas a record of something that has happened would need to be in writing.

Written and Spoken Communication in Business

Whether you communicate in writing or orally will depend on the circumstances, and to some extent on the person or people you are addressing. The main reasons for communicating orally are:

- **To have a discussion**. It is very difficult to hold a meaningful discussion by letter, memo or e-mail.

- **To receive instant feedback from your audience**. Speaking to someone means that you do not have to wait for their response. However, this can sometimes be a disadvantage; in some circumstances, a considered response might be better.

- **To be able to judge your audience's reaction to what you are saying**. This usually only applies in face-to-face communication, but it can sometimes be useful to be able to judge from your audience's comments, expressions or body language what they think of what you are saying and perhaps adapt your style or tone accordingly.

- **For speed**. Even the fastest typist or writer cannot match the speed at which we speak, so if you want to communicate something quickly, it might be better to do so orally.

- **If the person with whom you are communicating has initiated the conversation**. If you are responding to an oral request, for example, you are likely to do so orally, unless your response is so complex that it would be better explained in writing (see below).

The main reasons for communicating in writing are:

- **To retain a permanent record**. A conversation can be forgotten, misunderstood or even deliberately twisted. But if something is in writing (and if it is well written), everyone who reads it will be sure to get the right information. It also provides something to refer to if there is any dispute in the future. This is particularly important if the document constitutes a form of agreement, but it can also be useful in the case of a complaint.

- **To provide a basis for discussion**. We saw above that a discussion is usually best conducted orally, but it can be very useful for a discussion document to be available beforehand, setting out the facts of the case and perhaps giving the writer's own views and recommendations. This saves time, as it means that the meeting itself can discuss the implications and people's opinions, instead of having to go over the facts before any useful discussion can begin.

- **To clarify a complex subject**. Some subjects do not lend themselves easily to spoken communication. A graph or bar chart, for example, may be a better way of presenting figures, as you will see in Chapter 3, and it is easier to explain a confused situation in writing than orally (see Chapter 6).

- **To send the same message to a number of people**. If you want to give a number of people the same information (perhaps the date and venue of a meeting), then an e-mail or a circular memo or letter would be quicker and cheaper than speaking to each person individually.

- **To be able to think carefully about what you want to say**. You can plan your document and correct any errors before sending it out. It is easier to make a mistake when you are speaking spontaneously.

The differences between written and spoken English

There are, of course, significant differences between written and spoken English. Let us look at an example. Jane Lee, the Export Manager of John Smith & Sons Ltd, has had a meeting with a prospective agent in South America, Carlos Rodriguez. Below is a transcript of her verbal report on the meeting.

Jane Lee: I must say, I had a really good meeting with Mr Rodriguez. I think he might be the man for us. He seems to know the market very well, and he already does business all over South America.

Peter Morgan (Managing Director): Which countries exactly?

JL: Argentina, Venezuela, Chile, Colombia, Ecuador and Brazil mainly. He knows the import regulations for the different countries, but I would expect that – we wouldn't be considering him if he didn't! But he also seems to know things like who matters in each country, how they do business there, how we can avoid giving offence without knowing it, any problems there may be about payment, all that kind of thing. He is already agent for quite a few companies – Wilson Fabrics, Richmond Consumer Products and Simon Black Ltd – but they're all in competition with us, so it doesn't matter – sorry, I mean *none* of them is in competition with us. Oh by the way, I forgot to mention that he's based in Argentina, which is our fastest-expanding market in the area.

Sarah Brown (Financial Director): This all sounds too good to be true. Will he accept our usual commission?

JL: Yes, initially, but instead of being paid a fixed percentage, he would want to be able to negotiate his commission on a sliding scale eventually.

James Robinson (Operations Director): Sorry, Jane, what do you mean 'negotiate his commission on a sliding scale'?

JL: He would like his percentage commission to rise as our turnover in his territory increases. Now I know what some of you may be thinking – why pay him more than our other agents? Well, perhaps we should be paying them in the same way. After all, if Rodriguez increases our turnover significantly, then he probably *deserves* more.

Now look at what Jane might have *written*.

On 25 July I met Mr Carlos Rodriguez of Carlos Rodriguez Import SA, Buenos Aires, who has expressed an interest in becoming our agent in South America. I found the meeting both informative and productive. The main points we discussed are as follows.

Market penetration. He seems to know the South American market well, and he already does business in many of the countries there, in particular Argentina, Venezuela, Colombia, Ecuador and Brazil. He appears to have a sound knowledge of the business climate of each country. He is based in Argentina, which is our fastest-expanding market in the area.

Existing agencies. His existing agencies include Wilson Fabrics, Richmond Consumer Products and Simon Black Ltd. None of these companies is in competition with us; indeed their products complement ours, and no other agent has as good a track record as he does.

Commission. The commission arrangements he wants, however, are slightly different from our usual ones. Although he is prepared to accept our standard commission initially, he would like the percentage to rise as he increases our turnover in his territory – the details would have to be negotiated, but that is the principle behind his request. And as long as the turnover levels at which the new rates would operate are set at a sensible level, I believe the system would work to our advantage – he would have an additional incentive to work hard for us, and if the turnover does increase we could afford to pay him more. Of course, we might receive complaints from some of our other agents if they were to learn that we were paying him at a higher level, but it would be worth considering giving all our agents a similar incentive.

Can you see the differences between the two versions?

- **Spoken English uses unnecessary words and phrases**. When we speak, we generally use more words than we need to. Even when speaking, we should always try to be as concise as possible, but it is inevitable, unless we have gone to extremes in planning what we want to say, that we will introduce unnecessary and generally meaningless phrases such as:

  - 'I must say' – which adds nothing to the sense of the report.
  - 'Oh, by the way' – which means much the same as 'I forgot to mention'.
  - 'Really' – which is too vague to add anything to the word it goes with (what is the difference between a good meeting and a really good one?).

  These words and phrases do not matter in spoken English – indeed, they give us an opportunity to gather our thoughts, so they serve a useful purpose – but in writing they look sloppy and add to the length of the document.

- **Spoken English can be vague**. Jane talks about:

  - 'A really good meeting'. What does this mean? Was it productive, informative, enjoyable? Was the food good? She could mean any of these things.
  - 'All over South America'. In fact, as she indicates in her reply to Peter Morgan's question, she means 'in a number of the major countries', not 'all over'.
  - 'Things like who matters in each country, how they do business there ...' etc. This is a round about way of saying 'the business climate'.

  This vagueness does not matter when you are speaking, because your tone or gestures will indicate to your audience what you actually mean, or they can ask if anything is unclear. But when you are writing in business you need to be precise. Since your readers cannot ask you to clarify anything that is unclear, they will either make their own interpretations, which may be wrong, or ignore points they do not understand, which may give them an incomplete picture.

- **In spoken English you can go back and correct what you have said**. When you are speaking you can stop in midstream and correct yourself if you have said something wrong, or add in something you have forgotten. So Jane says:

  - 'Sorry, I mean' – when she realises she has said the opposite of what she means.
  - 'Oh, by the way, I forgot to mention' – when something occurs to her that she should have said earlier in the report.

When you are writing you should not have to go back and correct yourself. This kind of afterthought is fine in spoken English, but in written form it gives the document a disjointed appearance, making it difficult to follow.

- **When speaking you can respond to feedback from your audience**. As we have seen, this is one of the main reasons why you may decide to communicate orally rather than in writing. You can then explain things or amend your presentation accordingly.
  - When Peter Morgan asks Jane where Rodriguez does business, she clarifies her vague 'all over South America' statement.
  - In response to Sarah Brown's scepticism about his willingness to accept the company's usual terms, she is quick to point out that he will probably agree to them initially.
  - She explains the concept of a sliding scale of commission in response to James Robinson's question.
  - She sees from some people's reaction that they are still not convinced ('Now I know what some of you may be thinking'), so she introduces the point about the increase in turnover.

- **Spoken English often uses colloquialisms**. Slang is seldom acceptable in business English, unless you are speaking to a close friend, but using the odd colloquialism makes your speech sound less formal and constrained. So Jane says:
  - 'He might be the man for us'.
  - 'All that kind of thing'.

Colloquialisms are out of place in business documents, however. They look lazy, and they seldom have the precision of meaning that is needed.

Remember that, although a certain amount of informality is permissible when speaking, one general rule applies in all business communication, spoken and written: you should always be clear and precise.

EXERCISE 1

You work in the publicity office of a market town. You receive a phone call from Mr Lyndon Charles, who is thinking of visiting the town, but who wants to know what attractions you can offer. This is what you say in reply.

It really depends on what you're interested in and when you want to come. We've got a very good theatre, which usually has variety shows in summer and plays in winter. And if you're interested in cultural things, there's also a good museum and the church is famous for its carvings. And just outside town there's a medieval castle.

Oh, you've got young children, have you? Yes they may not be interested in the church and the museum. But they may like the castle, because it's supposed to be haunted. There's also a super play park, with a water feature. And within fairly easy driving distance there are two theme parks. The play park in town, by the way, is free, but you'd obviously have to pay at the theme parks. Of course, they would also have fun on the beaches nearby – the nearest is about ten minutes' drive. Yes it's sandy, not pebbly.

And do you like walking? You do? Well the countryside around here is beautiful, and there are some lovely walks through the woods – and also along the coast, of course, although there's a lot of up and down along this stretch of the Coast Path.

Mr Charles asks if you can put all this information in writing. Write him a letter summarising your telephone conversation.

Business and Other Styles of Communication

Not all styles of communication are the same; a style that suits one set of circumstances might be totally wrong for another. The way you communicate, even the language you use, will be very different, for example, if you are writing a novel, or e-mailing or speaking to a friend, from the style you would adopt for business.

Business and literary styles

There are three main differences in style between a business document and a work of literature.

- **Literary writing is usually descriptive**. A novel writer would spend some time creating an atmosphere, giving some background detail. If the account of Jane Lee's meeting with Carlos Rodriguez were part of a novel, for example, there would almost certainly be a description of the restaurant where they met, and of Rodriguez himself. This kind of description is out of place in business writing. Your readers do not have time to read descriptions which have no real bearing on the subject. Where description is necessary, it should be factual and objective, not flowery and subjective.

- **Literary writing uses direct speech**. In a novel, the author will describe what people say in the exact words they used – direct speech. This is another way of involving the reader. But you would very seldom use direct speech in business writing – it tends to be too long-winded. People want to absorb the information you are giving as quickly and easily as possible, so give them a summary of what was said, not the actual words.

- **Literary writing introduces personal feelings**. A work of literature will describe the characters' feelings about others and their surroundings – that is part of the skill of telling a story. So a novel might describe how Jane reacted to Rodriguez on a personal level, what she thought of the meal, etc. These feelings have no place in business writing; they simply clutter up the document unnecessarily. Your opinions might be important, depending on the nature of your document, but your feelings are irrelevant.

What this means is that business communication should be as brief and uncluttered as possible while still getting across the information you want to impart.

Business and personal styles

Although business English is much less formal and more conversational than it used to be, it is still different from the language you might use in personal communication. There are four main differences.

- **Personal communication uses slang**. As we have seen, a bit of colloquial language is quite acceptable when speaking in a business context, but outright slang is not. So, for example, Jane Lee says of Carlos Rodriguez, 'He might be the man for us', which is acceptable, although it is something of a colloquialism. In a personal letter, she might have said, 'He's got what it takes' or 'He's the guy for the job'; neither of these expressions would be acceptable in business, even when speaking – unless, of course, the person you are speaking or writing to is a personal friend with whom you have a very informal business relationship.

- **Personal communication is subjective.** When you are writing or speaking to a friend, you are talking about what *you* have been doing and thinking – that is the main reason for writing. So your letter is likely to be full of references to your own actions, feelings and reactions. Therefore in a personal letter or conversation, Jane might say, 'I could find it very easy to work with him', or 'I was really pleased when he agreed to our terms', etc. But business communication should be more objective – the only relevance your actions or feelings have is their impact on your business and the person you are addressing.

- **Business correspondence is not read for pleasure.** Very often when writing personal letters or e-mails, our aim is to give pleasure to the recipient. So we might introduce funny or interesting anecdotes. In business correspondence you should not try to entertain your audience. People read business documents to gain information as quickly and easily as possible; they read other things for pleasure.

- **Personal communication sometimes exaggerates or uses euphemisms.** It is not uncommon for statements in personal letters or conversations to stretch the truth a little, in order to show someone in a good light, or perhaps to spare the feelings of the audience. Most of us do it at some time: we might say for example, 'I have left my job' rather than 'I have been made redundant'. So in a personal letter, Jane might try to give the impression that she charmed Rodriguez into accepting the company's usual commission when in fact he agreed very reluctantly to do so, and only on certain conditions. In business, you should give the facts objectively.

The Three Rules of Business Communication

Business communication should be:

- clear and precise

- brief and uncluttered

- direct and to the point

EXERCISE 2

Below is the text of an e-mail to a friend about a business trip to Germany. What would you need to change in order to make it acceptable as a brief business report?

I had a fantastic trip to Berlin last week. Horst Kuhn, the guy I was doing business with, was great, and we got on really well. He took me to this amazing restaurant one evening for dinner, and then on to a club, where we met up with some of his friends.

The business side went well, too. His company is very interested in a joint venture with us, to supply financial software to banks and other financial institutions across Europe. Horst reckons that with our complementary markets (they do a lot in Eastern Europe, while we're particularly strong in Scandinavia, France and Holland) we could clean up if we joined forces. The terms he suggested were a bit tricky (he's a persuasive guy, and was trying to get me to agree to them having a 60 per cent share) but I stuck to my guns and managed to persuade him to ask his Board to consider equal shares.

There's still a lot of work to do, but I think we'll get a really good deal out of this. At the risk of blowing my own trumpet, I reckon I'm capable of getting our Board to take the idea seriously.

CHAPTER 2
Planning what you are going to say

Whatever the form of your communication, it is important to plan what you are going to say in advance. Of course, when you are speaking your plan cannot be too detailed, as you do not know how the conversation is going to develop – you should certainly not try to plan everything you are going to say. You have probably come across telesales staff who have been told exactly what to say in any given circumstances; the conversation becomes rather stilted and they are at a bit of a loss if it deviates from their script. But you should nevertheless have a good general idea of what you want to say and how you will express it. And in written communication, you need not spend a great deal of time on a very routine letter, but even that will need *some* planning.

There will, of course, be times when you cannot plan ahead – when answering the telephone, for example. If you are not able to find the information you need immediately, then it might be better to promise to phone the other person back, and then plan what you want to say once you have it to hand.

Why Plan?

You should plan what you are going to say to ensure that:

- you say everything that has to be said

- the information you give is correct

- your arguments are logically expressed

- you use the right language to suit your purpose

- you are not emotional

It is just possible that you might achieve what you want without proper planning, but it is highly unlikely, and you would certainly not achieve this every time if you always came to the subject 'cold'.

Your Reasons for Writing or Speaking

Before you plan what you are going to say, you should ask yourself the following questions:

- Should you be writing or speaking to the person concerned?
- Are you addressing the right person? You can waste a lot of time being passed from one person in the organisation to another if you address the wrong person initially, and in the case of a written document it could be lost or ignored in the process.

Once you have satisfied yourself on these points, you should ask yourself two further questions.

- Should anyone else be aware of what you want to say? All your planning can come to nothing if you do not address everyone who needs the information you are giving.
- Do you need a reply? If you do, and you do not let the other person know, you will have failed to achieve your purpose. (See Chapter 3 for more on how to ensure that a correspondent knows what you expect him or her to do.)

Finally, there are two more questions.

- What is your purpose in writing or speaking?
- What do you want to achieve?

Let us look at these two in more detail.

What is your purpose?

This might seem an unnecessary question. After all, you would not be getting in touch with the other person if you did not have a reason. But it is important to clarify in your own mind just what your purpose is, and to bear it in mind as you write or speak. Look at the letter below. Can you see what is wrong with it?

JAMES LONG & CO

Furniture Manufacturers and Suppliers

125 Broadlands Road

Valley Industrial Estate

Storton

ST4 5UV

Tel. 01234 567890

12 December 20XX

Mrs J. Brown
Cliff Hotel
Marine Drive
Oldport

Dear Mrs Brown

I was very sorry to see from your letter of 3 December that the legs of one of the occasional tables supplied to you recently are coming off.

I have undertaken a thorough investigation of the problem, and I have discovered what went wrong. It appears that a batch of the fixing brackets we use for that particular range was faulty. Our quality control procedures picked up the fault soon after we took delivery, and that batch was put to one side for return to the manufacturer.

Unfortunately, we have recently taken on a new member of staff, and he mistook the faulty brackets for the batch that had been laid out for him to use. Our quality control procedures at the end of the production process are only designed to find faults in our own workmanship, assuming that the pre-production checks will have picked up faults in bought-in components. ▶

As a result of your letter I have changed our procedures, and we now check all our finished products for faults both in our own workmanship and in bought-in components. We now also ensure that any items to be returned to our suppliers are kept well away from the production line.

Yours sincerely

Donald Benson
Production Manager

It is a good letter, but it is not suitable for the purpose for which it was written. Donald Benson obviously knew why he was writing to Mrs Brown – to answer her complaint. But he did not have that thought clearly in his mind when he planned his letter. The result is that he gives a full explanation of how the problem arose, but he does not actually answer her complaint. Mrs Brown is not likely to be interested in the details of how her table came to be faulty. What she wants to know is what the company is going to do about it – and Donald does not tell her.

Only by keeping in mind *why* you are writing or speaking to someone can you be sure that what you say is relevant both to the subject matter and to the person you are addressing. What Donald says is relevant to the subject, but not to the person. He should have kept the explanation to the minimum, apologised for the error and offered some remedy. This underlines the importance of planning when you are about to speak to someone; it can be very easy to be side-tracked, and to forget your purpose.

This is not to say that the sort of detail Donald gives here would never be appropriate. If he had been asked by the Managing Director to explain how the table came to be faulty and how he intended to ensure that a similar problem did not occur again, he might have sent him a memo or e-mail exactly along the lines of the last three paragraphs of his letter. In this case, his purpose would be to explain the problem and his solution, so the detail would be extremely relevant, both to the subject and to the person he is addressing.

It is easier to plan what you are going to say if you only have one purpose. You can concentrate on getting your content, style, tone and wording right for that purpose. But there will be times – usually when writing letters, but occasionally when speaking on the telephone – when you might have to cover two subjects in the same document or conversation. You might, for example, need to explain a change in distribution arrangements to a customer, but also to chase an overdue payment. It would be silly to write two letters or make two calls, so you would cover both subjects in one. The best way to handle this situation is to separate the two subjects, and to deal completely with one before introducing the other. There will need to be some device to link the two subjects, but otherwise they are best planned separately. The letter below shows how this is done. The two subjects are dealt with in two separate sections, separately planned, and linked with the phrase 'While I am writing'. Exactly the same principle applies to a conversation: you should plan the two subjects separately, then deal with one (including any queries that arise) before moving on to the next, linking the two with a phrase like 'While I am on the phone'.

COLOURSCHEME PAINTS LTD
53 King's Way, Topperton, AB23 4CD
Tel. 01678 901234 Fax 01678 9013435

12 March 20XX

Mr Patrick Swan
Proprietor
The Paint and Paper Shop
4 Queen Street
Winterborough
ST12 3UV

Dear Mr Swan

You will be pleased to know that, as from 1 April, we will be instituting a new, improved distribution service.

The first change is in our own internal systems. We are now able to turn your orders around on the day they are received, so that the goods are ready for despatch the following morning. The second is in our carriers. We will be using XYZ Haulage Ltd, who offer a guaranteed 24-hour delivery service. The combination of these two changes means that you should in future receive delivery of your goods no later than 48 hours after we receive your order.

While I am writing, perhaps I could mention that there is an amount of £156.79 overdue on your account. We do not appear to have received payment of our invoice No. 09876 of 20 January. As you know, our terms are 30 days from the date of invoice, so this payment is now well overdue. I would be grateful if you would let me have your cheque for this amount by return of post.

Yours sincerely

Michael Milton
Sales Manager

What do you want to achieve?

Do not confuse your purpose with what you want to achieve; the two are related but different. For example, Donald Benson wrote to Mrs Brown to answer her complaint – that was his purpose, although as we have seen the letter he wrote was not right for that purpose. What he wanted to achieve was to satisfy her, and to make her feel better about the company. So your purpose will dictate what goes into your letter, while the outcome you want will dictate the style and tone you use.

So in addition to keeping your purpose in mind while you are planning what you are going to say, you should also keep in mind what you want to achieve. Look at the e-mail below sent by a company's Accountant to the Purchase Ledger Clerk.

Your Purpose and What You Want to Achieve

Here are some examples to illustrate the difference between the purpose of your communication and what you want to achieve.

- The purpose of a sales letter is to tell people about your product or service. What you want to achieve is a sale.

- The purpose of a complaining telephone call is to point out an error or fault. What you want to achieve is the correction of that error or fault, or else compensation.

- The purpose of a credit control letter is to chase an overdue account. What you want to achieve is payment.

- The purpose of a report on the advantages and disadvantages of different work practices is to inform the decision-makers of the options available. What you want to achieve is acceptance of the most efficient option.

To: Brian Carter
From: Sandra Jones
Subject: Payment of invoices

The Purchasing Manager has complained to me that he is unable to maintain reasonable stocks of many items because we are constantly being put on stop by one supplier or another. This in turn is having an adverse effect on sales. This complaint has put me in an extremely embarrassing position, as I have been criticising the Sales Department in management meetings for their poor performance.

There is absolutely no excuse for holding up payments, especially to major suppliers. Your instructions are to pay all invoices as soon as they are cleared. This you have clearly failed to do on a number of occasions, and I want to know why, and what you intend to do to ensure that it does not happen again. Please give me a report on the situation by Thursday.

Sandra Jones is quite clear about the purpose of her e-mail: to get Brian Carter to see why the company is so slow in paying its accounts. But is she as clear about what she wants to achieve and how to achieve it? What she wants to achieve is to get to the bottom of the problem and ensure that the process is speeded up. But will this memo achieve that aim? Below is an alternative version of the same e-mail.

To: Brian Carter
From: Sandra Jones
Subject: Payment of invoices

The Purchasing Manager has complained to me that he is unable to maintain reasonable stocks of many items because we are constantly being put on stop by one supplier or another. This in turn is having an adverse effect on sales.

Something is obviously going wrong with our payment system, because as you know we should be paying invoices as soon as they are cleared. The problem may be that they are not being cleared quickly enough, or there may be delays within our department. Either way, I think we need to look at the system to see how we can speed things up.

Could you look into the problem for me, and find out what has gone wrong? I would like to discuss your conclusions, together with any suggestions you have for improving the situation, on Thursday.

If you were Brian Carter, which e-mail would you prefer to receive? Which would be more likely to make you conduct a thorough investigation, and which would simply put you on the defensive? Apart from its obvious rudeness (and as we shall see, rudeness will very seldom achieve the objective you want), the first is less likely to achieve Sandra's aim for the following reasons.

- The first e-mail makes an accusation, so that Brian is likely to act defensively and look for excuses rather than explanations. The second is not accusatory, so that even if Brian finds that he is at fault, he is unlikely to be afraid to admit it.
- The first assumes that the fault lies within Brian's area of responsibility, so he might look no further in his investigations. The second does not make this assumption, so he is encouraged to look at all the stages an invoice goes through, including authorisation, for example, resulting in a more thorough investigation.
- The first gives him an order, so that his reaction might be to do just as much as is required to satisfy Sandra and get him out of trouble and no more. The second invites his co-operation so that, as the person closest to the payment system, he is encouraged to come up with recommendations for improving it.

EXERCISE 3

Look again at the letter from Donald Benson to Mrs Brown on pages 9–10. Rewrite it, bearing in mind both Donald's purpose in writing, and what he should have wanted to achieve.

Getting the Right Reaction

Who is your audience?

The first step towards achieving the outcome you want is to get to know your audience. The style, the tone, even the content of your communication will depend very much on who you are addressing. First, your audience can be categorised according to their knowledge of your business.

- There are people who will know very little, such as members of the public for example.
- There are those who will know something about the business you are in, but not about your particular organisation, such as your customers.
- There are those who will not only know about the business you are in, but also about your organisation, such as your colleagues or an agent.

The way you write or speak, and in particular the language you use, will depend on which of these categories your audience falls into. With someone who knows nothing about your business or your organisation, you would want to use everyday language that a lay person will understand. With someone who knows something about the business generally but not about your organisation, you might use some jargon that is specific to that area, but not words and phrases that have a specific meaning only in your organisation. And with someone who knows both the business and your organisation, you are likely to use both general business terms and jargon that is specific to your organisation.

EXERCISE 4

You are a publisher. Below are three ways of reporting that a book is no longer available.

1. *Practical Goosekeeping* is now reporting O/P. We are considering either a reprint or a new edition, but we cannot make a decision until we have a pre-production costings and proposal form. In the meantime we are recording dues.

2. I am afraid that *Practical Goosekeeping* is out of stock at present, although we are considering reprinting it. I shall keep your order on file, and let you know the position as soon as we have made a decision.

3. I am afraid that *Practical Goosekeeping* is currently out of print. A reprint or new edition is under consideration, and we are therefore recording your order on our dues file.

Which would you use for the following types of correspondent?

(a) a member of the public

(b) a bookseller

(c) one of your colleagues

But it is not just a question of categorising your audience according to how much they know about your business. There are other factors to be taken into account if you are to suit your communication to your audience. To help you gain a better understanding of the people you will be addressing, ask yourself the following questions:

- Do they know anything about the subject you will be speaking or writing about, or are there ideas or technical terms that will need explaining?

- What is your relationship with them? Is it formal or informal?

- Are they expecting to hear from you? If not, will they be interested in what you have to say?

- What do *they* believe is important? For example, if you are presenting a report suggesting that your organisation sets up a staff social club, you should not simply say how good it would be for staff morale if the person to whom you are addressing it is more concerned with profit margins than staff morale. You would be better off pointing out how cheap it would be to do, and then suggesting that the improvement in staff morale could bring a further improvement in commitment and productivity.

- What are they likely to agree to readily, and what will they need to be persuaded about? This will affect the order in which you present your points, and the space you devote to them.

Once you know what your audience is like, keep that in mind as you plan what you are going to say. Try to see what you are going to say from their point of view.

Deciding How to Address Your Audience

- How technical can you be – how much do the people you are addressing know about the business you are in and your organisation?

- Will you need to explain any terms?

- Should you use formal or informal language?

- Will your audience be interested in what you have to say, or will you have to engage their interest?

- What is important to them?

- What expressions or phrases are likely to appeal to them and make them take notice?

Choose the right language

Once you know your audience, you can decide what sort of language you need to use. Should it be technical or non-technical, formal or informal, simple or complex?

The examples given in Exercise 4 show how the degree of 'technicality' can vary according to the audience you are addressing. There are similar variations in the degree of informality you can introduce. Look at the letter below.

SQUIRES AND CORNISH
3 The Square
Marchester
MA1 9YZ
Tel: 01345 678901

1 February 20XX

Ms Marian Matthews
Alpha Products Ltd
4 King Street
London
SW14 1AZ

Dear Ms Matthews

I would like to apply to act as an agent for your company in northern Europe. We are a small but expanding partnership with a substantial volume of business representing a variety of companies in Scandinavia, the Netherlands, Belgium and Germany.

Indeed, our business is expanding to such an extent that we are planning to take on more representatives in the near future. In looking for new companies to act for, we were very interested to see the variety of products you offer; it appears to us that your range could complement those we currently represent. I also notice that you do not appear to have any sales representation in these important markets, and I believe that we could substantially increase your sales there.

▶

I would be happy to travel to London to meet you and discuss terms if you would like to pursue the matter further. I can, of course, provide suitable references should you require them.

Yours sincerely

Julia Squires
Senior Partner

This is a formal letter, using formal language, which suits the audience. Julia Squires does not know Marian Matthews and her letter is a formal application. Despite the current trend towards more informality in business usage, this is an instance when a certain degree of formality is called for.

Now look at the following letter.

ACME ADVERTISING
35 Albany Street
Queenstown
QT5 6XY
01987 487236

24 April 20XX

James King
Managing Director
Paragon Interiors
4 Brownhill Drive
Queenstown
QT4 5AZ

Dear James

Many thanks for the lunch on Tuesday. It was, as usual, a most enjoyable meal.

I have done a rough costing on the brochure we discussed. I will, of course, send you the formal estimate when our financial people have completed it, but my first reaction is that we should be able to meet your needs within the budget you have set, with one proviso. As I said over lunch, a company like yours needs to project an upmarket image, and that calls for a high-quality production. So rather than producing a 16-page brochure and having to compromise on quality I would suggest doing eight pages, highly illustrated, on quality art paper. Of course, there is another alternative – you could increase your budget!

I will be in touch with the formal estimate shortly, but I felt you might want to know my thoughts before your board meeting on Monday.

With kind regards

Yours sincerely

Fiona Thompson

This is a very different kind of communication. The language Fiona uses would not be appropriate for Julia's letter, but it just right for the kind of communication it is – an informal letter to someone she obviously knows well, with whom she has just had lunch, and with whom she enjoys a good business relationship. Can you notice the differences?

- Julia uses expressions like:
  - indeed
  - pursue the matter further
  - should you decide
- Fiona says things like:
  - many thanks (rather than 'thank you very much')
  - our financial people (rather than 'our Accounts Department')
  - I felt you might want to know my thoughts (rather than 'I thought I would give you a provisional estimate')

Simple expressions like these can give your communication a completely different tone.

The nature of your audience will also dictate how simple your language should be. Business English should never be over-complicated, but you can sometimes introduce fairly complex concepts if you feel that your audience will be able to understand them. Imagine that you are giving a presentation to your colleagues on the possibility of developing a new market in an imaginary country. In your assessment of the country, you might include a passage like the following:

> There are a lot of risks in trying to open up a market in Sulanesia. In the first place, as this graph indicates, it has a monocultural economy. In 20XX/Y bananas made up 85% of the country's official exports. They also account for a large proportion of its Gross National Product – I can't give you the precise percentage, because a lot of economic activity takes place in the informal sector. So it's very vulnerable to fluctuations in world prices.

> It's also very unstable politically. There have been five coups, two coup attempts and one so-called 'palace revolution' in the last ten years, and the present president's position is looking increasingly shaky.

In talking like this, you would be assuming quite a good knowledge of current affairs and economic terminology among your audience. Only someone well versed in world affairs would understand concepts such as 'monocultural economy', 'Gross National Product', 'the informal sector' and 'palace revolution'.

If you were unsure of your colleagues' level of understanding of such terms, you would have to find other ways of explaining these ideas. However, it is unwise to talk down too obviously to your audience. If you are not sure whether they will understand a particular point or phrase, you can get round the difficulty by explaining it, but prefacing your explanation with something like 'As you will know' or 'I am sure you're aware'. In that way, those who are aware will not feel that you are insulting their intelligence, and those who are not still have the concepts explained.

Whatever language you decide is appropriate for your audience, there are two things you should *never* do, in any circumstances.

- **You should never be rude or abrupt**. Even if you are making a complaint, make it politely. Even a final demand for payment can be expressed in courteous terms. Some managers seem to think that memos and e-mails to junior colleagues do not matter, and that they can be as rude as they like. This was obviously Sandra Jones's view when she wrote the e-mail on page 12. But rudeness is not only bad manners; it will not get the reaction you want.

- **You should never be emotional**. It is important in business that you should present facts and reasoned arguments, not emotional outbursts. Of course, you may feel angry about something, but if possible wait until your anger has cooled before you write or speak – and if you have to react immediately to something the other person says, then take a deep breath and try to calm down before responding!

EXERCISE 5

Below is an extract from a sales letter about a range of soft furnishings. What kind of audience do you think it is aimed at, and how would you change it to suit a different audience?

Fanfare Style is pleased to introduce the latest collection to emerge from their studios – an original range of soft furnishings that will add a touch of elegance to any room. There are stylish designs to suit any decor, in a variety of fabrics.

Checking your facts

As we saw in Chapter 1, it is important that your business communications should be precise. This precision applies not only to their meaning, but also to their content. Do ensure that your facts are accurate, and that you do not leave out any relevant information.

It is sloppy to provide inaccurate information, and it will reflect badly on you. But it can also cause other problems. Look at the e-mail below, sent by a company's Systems Director to his colleagues.

To: All Directors
From: Alan Walters
Subject: New Appointment

I have been concerned for some time that we are not getting the most out of our computer systems. This is no reflection on the staff in my department, all of whom work extremely hard. It is simply that we do not have the number of properly trained staff we need if we are to serve other departments well.

Departments are currently having to wait up to six months for any new development in their systems. The Production Department, for example, wanted a very minor modification to the program for producing cost prices but had to wait four months because my staff were too busy to make the necessary changes earlier. And when we finally got round to producing the program the Accounts Department wanted to enable it to produce more sophisticated analyses of sales and costs, it needed a great deal of debugging, because I had to allocate it to someone who did not have the right knowledge; Celia Brown, the only person in the department with experience of that kind of work, was involved in another, more urgent, project. And of course the time I had to spend debugging the program could have been spent on other, more productive work.

These are just two of the most recent problems caused by the lack of staff, and both of them have, I understand, caused a number of difficulties for the departments concerned, and a loss of efficiency all round.

I therefore think that we should, as a matter of urgency, make a new appointment to the Systems Department, that of Project Leader. He or she would report to the Systems Manager, and would be responsible for new development work. I would like to discuss this at our next meeting.

It is fine as it stands, providing that all the information is correct. But let us assume that Alan got the projects confused, and that it was another program that needed debugging – the Accounts Department program had only just been completed, so he did not know whether it needed debugging or not. People reading the e-mail who were aware of this (the Financial Director, for example) might well become suspicious of the other arguments Alan puts forward. He would begin to lose credibility; his reasons for taking on a project leader would still be valid, but he would have more difficulty in convincing the other directors.

Ensure also that you have *all* the relevant facts. You can construct a most convincing argument if you are selective in the information you use, but it can be completely destroyed by someone who has all the facts. For example, Alan's argument in favour of employing a project leader would be considerably weakened if one of his colleagues were to point out that the current rate of new development is a short-term phenomenon, while the company brings its systems up to date. In that case, the Board could quite legitimately argue that a better alternative would be to hire a consultant for a few months to cope with the extra work.

Assembling and Ordering Your Information and Arguments

Now you are ready to start the actual planning process, and this involves assembling your information, working out the most logical way of presenting it and deciding how you are going to express it.

Planning Your Communication

The stages you need to go through in planning what you are going to say are:

- Assemble your information and the arguments you are going to use in presenting your case.

- Write an outline of what you are going to say.

- Organise the outline into a logical order, so that you move naturally from one point to the next.

- If you are preparing a written document, compile your first draft.

- Edit this draft into the final version.

Of course, not all business communications need the same amount of attention. If you were writing a short, fairly simple e-mail, you would not go through the processes in detail, although you would be well advised to skip through them mentally. And if you were preparing for a telephone call or a meeting, then you should not write out exactly what you were going to say, as that would make your conversation sound very false, but you should at least prepare an outline of the main points you wanted to make, and the order in which you wanted to raise them. On the other hand, if you were compiling a long report or a presentation, you would be foolish not to devote a lot of time and attention to your preparation.

Assembling your information

Do collect all the information you need before you write your document, go to your meeting or make your telephone call. If you are answering a complaint or enquiry, do you have the answers to *all* the points raised? If you are writing a report, have you considered *all* the arguments before reaching your conclusion? If you are making an enquiry, do you know *exactly* what you are trying to find out? You must make your purpose in writing or speaking quite clear, and if there is likely to be any confusion, it is best to communicate in writing; as we have seen, a conversation can be misunderstood.

EXERCISE 6

Below is a memo regarding the introduction of new working practices in an office. What do you think is wrong with it? How would you rewrite it to make it clearer?

From: Satish Chaudri, Managing Director
To: All department managers
Date: 3 April 20XX

WORK BREAKS

A number of people have commented on the fact that staff seem to be away from their desks rather a lot. I am not against people taking breaks in principle – after all we should be able to trust our staff to get their work done without having to watch them all the time. But we cannot just allow people to wander off whenever they wish – we do need to keep some check on the amount they work, don't we? Of course, if we try to restrict their breaks, there might be some opposition, and it could affect staff morale. But do you think we might consider some system where people ask permission before leaving their workstations? And of course we need to consider what the union's attitude would be. Please let me have a report on the situation as you see it.

When you have all the information you need, you can start marshalling your arguments and the points you want to make. You must present what you want to say in a logical, coherent way, otherwise you will either lose your audience through boredom or misunderstanding, or not make your point effectively. There are two ways of making a convincing point, both equally valid:

- **By deduction**. This involves reasoning from one statement to another to reach a conclusion – *deducing* the answer. For example, an employee of a furniture manufacturer might want to make a case for changing their timber supplier. Their report outlining the reasons might include the following:

Whenever our machines are left idle, we lose money. Continuity of production is vital to our business, and this depends on a guaranteed supply of raw materials. Our present supplier is unable to guarantee supplies of the woods we need, and has let us down on several occasions. We therefore cannot guarantee continuity of production.

This passage contains two statements on which the whole argument rests – the *premises*: 'continuity of production depends on a guaranteed supply of raw materials' and 'our present supplier cannot guarantee supplies'. By a process of deduction the writer concludes that 'we cannot guarantee continuity of production'. And if both the premises are true, then the argument cannot be faulted.

But beware of false deductions. Look at the following extract:

Continuity of production depends on a guaranteed supply of raw materials. The new supplier can guarantee supplies. With the new supplier, therefore, we will be able to guarantee continuity of production.

This is a false deduction, because a guaranteed supply is only *one* of the factors necessary for continuity of production.

You can see the difference between these two arguments if you change the first premise to read 'Continuity of production depends, *amongst other things*, on a guaranteed supply of raw materials.' In the first argument, the second premise ('The supplier is unable to guarantee supplies') nullifies one of the 'things' on which continuity depends, so the whole continuity is nullified. In the second argument, the second premise ('The new supplier *can* guarantee supplies') confirms one of the 'things' *but not all of them*. Unless the others are also confirmed, the continuity cannot be confirmed.

- **By induction**. This involves reasoning from your experience, or from your own investigation. Unlike a conclusion arrived at by deduction, one arrived at by induction cannot usually be proved beyond any doubt. But you should be able to show that:
  - the conclusion is reasonable given the information at your disposal
  - your knowledge or experience covers a wide area or sample
  - the sample on which you are basing your conclusion is typical of the circumstances, people, areas, etc. of the whole group

For example, a report on a company's sales force might include the following:

Our sales this year are down by 10 per cent on last year, and I believe the reason is that the sales force is not working as efficiently as it should. I have examined the records of a sample of ten representatives, and in each case I found deficiencies.

This is argument by induction. The writer's conclusion, that the sales force is not working as efficiently as it should, is based on the information gained during their investigation. It cannot be proved beyond any doubt, but it is a valid assumption to make, given the results of the investigation.

But it is only valid if it fulfils the criteria listed above. What if the drop in sales was the result of production difficulties, not a drop in orders – in other words, the company had the orders but was unable to fulfil them? In that case the conclusion would not be reasonable given the information available, and would not satisfy the first criterion. And if the sales force consisted of 40 representatives, then the records of only ten of them would not be a large enough sample, so the conclusion would not satisfy the

second criterion. If there were only 20, then ten would be a reasonable sample. But if the ten chosen were the ones with the worst records, then they would not be typical, and the conclusion would not satisfy the third conclusion.

So whether you are arguing by deduction or induction, it is very easy to be led into making false conclusions. And if your audience picks up on the fact that one of your conclusions is false, it will at best weaken your argument and at worst destroy it.

Writing an outline of what you are going to say

There are three main ways of writing an outline. It does not matter which you use – you might even combine techniques. Try them out and see which suits you best. The three methods are:

- **Charting**. Also called a spidergram, this used to be a fairly common method of writing an outline, but has become less popular recently, as it is not easy to do on a computer. It involves doing a rough diagram, with the main idea in the centre and ideas for sections or paragraphs coming off it. It is rather like brainstorming – one idea leads to another. Then you can order your points in a logical sequence, as suggested below.
- **Listing**. This is perhaps the most popular method of outlining what you want to say. It simply involves making a list of the points you want to make, in no particular order. Do not try to combine two points on the same line – it only complicates the next stage. If you want to be sophisticated, you can use a different-coloured pen to write particularly important points, or you can use a highlighter. The main thing is to list anything you think might be relevant – you can always leave something out later if you decide it is not important enough, or does not fit in. Then you can order your points in a logical sequence simply by numbering them. Below is an example of a list outline for a letter giving a customer a quotation.

    Samples of different fabrics enclosed.
    10% off all orders to the end of March.
    Each design specific to us.
    Design 41 available in blue or green.
    Design 53 available in grey/blue or brown/beige.
    Design 62 available in red only.
    Design 67 available in black/white or blue/white.
    All designs the same price.
    Prices: £10 per metre up to 50 metres
             £9 per metre 50–100 metres
             £7.50 per metre over 100 metres
    Over 200 metres, prices negotiable.
    Terms 30 days from date of delivery.
    Design 18 no longer available.
    Prices include carriage.

- **Freewriting**. This is probably the least used technique, and it is not one that I would usually recommend. Some people do prefer it, however, so you might want to try it. It involves writing down everything that comes to you, without stopping but always bearing in mind your aim and your audience. Put everything down that you can think of, no matter how trivial, and do not worry about grammar or construction at this stage. If you know that your construction is wrong, leave it but mark it to come back to. If you cannot think of the right word, leave a blank space or use a less suitable word but mark it. If you need to check any facts, mark them too, and go back. Then go through what you have written, highlighting what is important and deleting anything that should, on second thoughts, be left out. Then rearrange the text into a logical order.

Making your points flow logically

It is very important that you sort your points into a logical order. Unless you present your arguments in such a way that your audience is led easily from one point to the next, you will not be communicating effectively.

Achieving a Logical Sequence

There are five ways of assembling your points so that they flow logically:

- in chronological order

- building up an argument by deduction, induction or both

- in the same order as the document to which you are replying

- in ascending order of importance

- in descending order of importance

Deciding which is the best order for your purposes depends on what you want to say. In some cases, only one order is suitable, but in others you may be able to choose one of two or three options. You need to think carefully about which one suits the subject, the audience and the outcome you want to achieve.

If you are writing about a complex sequence of events (or speaking about them, although it can be very difficult to make a complex point orally), then a chronological approach is almost certainly going to be the best. Look at the letter below.

J. PETERSON & CO
Paper Merchants

14 Union Road
Kingston Magna
Barsetshire
BZ21 0YX
Tel. 01902 134567

8 April 20XX

Mr Roy Thompson
Clark & Co plc
Devonshire Street
Bath
BA3 4ZY

Dear Mr Thompson

I am extremely concerned about our order No. 456239 of 18 January for 20 laptop computers. You may recall that we asked for delivery on 31 January.   ▶

On 7 February I had to chase you because the machines had not been delivered as requested.

On 20 February, nearly three weeks after our requested delivery date, the machines were delivered. Unfortunately, only 15 of them had all the software we requested installed on them. All the others had something missing. I therefore telephoned you on 21 February and complained. You promised to send another five laptops with the correct software, and collect the others.

On 4 March we had still not received the replacement laptops, so I telephoned you and asked you to deliver them as soon as possible.

On 11 March the replacement machines were delivered, but two of them proved to be faulty. I therefore telephoned you on 13 March, and you promised to send an engineer to check them.

He had not arrived by 22 March, so I telephoned again. This time you said you would send two replacement machines and collect the faulty ones.

On 29 March, when they had not arrived, I chased again, and was told by your secretary that they were on the way. They have still not arrived.

We have been waiting almost three months now for our order to be fulfilled correctly. I would be grateful if you could telephone me within the next two days to tell me what you are going to do about the situation. In view of the delay, and the effect on our business, I would also like to discuss the question of compensation.

Yours sincerely

Emma Porter

Systems Manager

By setting out her points in this way, Emma makes it quite clear just how badly Clark & Co. have treated her. You can follow the sequence of events, and you can see why certain actions were taken at certain times. If she were to try to present her points in order of importance, it would not have the same impact – indeed, it would probably simply muddy the waters. And you can see that she really needs to make a written complaint in order to convey the full extent of Clark & Co.'s faults – Roy Thompson would not be able to absorb all the information if she had just telephoned him.

If you are trying to persuade someone to take a certain course of action, then it is usually best to try to build up an argument. Look at the memo below.

Date: 24 January 20XX
To: All Directors
From: Ken Jameson
Re: Appointment of an Administration Manager

We have now reduced the applicants for the above post to a shortlist of three. I have interviewed all three and they have gone through an assessment centre. All three are extremely well qualified for the post, but in very different ways. The following are my own assessments of the candidates.

Judy Pearce has had a great deal of experience of managing people, as well as some administrative experience. From my interview and the assessment results, she appears to be a dominant personality, with firm ideas of how she would run the department. She tends to 'lead from the front'. She does not suffer fools gladly, but is very conscientious. I would expect her to ask a lot of her staff, but no more than she is prepared to do herself.

Hassan Ahmed has little experience of managing people, but he has a very sound knowledge of administrative practices, and is well informed about the latest developments in the field. He shows every sign of being able to develop the requisite 'people management' skills and would probably become a very committed manager, leading by example and by his knowledge of the subject.

Michael Hopwood has had a great deal of experience in managing a large department, and has the necessary skills in that area. He has no direct administrative knowledge, although he is currently on a course to acquire some. He appears to believe in a more 'democratic' style of management than the other two, involving his whole department in decisions that concern them. His assessment report indicates, however, that he is not afraid to assert his authority when the need arises.

All three candidates therefore have strengths and weaknesses. We obviously need a manager who can motivate the department. We also need to take into account the present situation, both in the department and in the organisation as a whole. The staff in the department are of a very high calibre, and are prepared to commit themselves fully to the job. The organisation as a whole is committed to the greater involvement of staff in the decision-making process. Administrative skills can be learned, but the right approach to staff management is something which to a large extent cannot be taught. I believe that Michael Hopwood has the right management approach as well as the ability to learn the administrative skills. I therefore recommend that he be appointed to the post.

Ken Jameson presents his assessments of the candidates, arrived at by a process of induction. He then argues, by deduction, for the candidate of his choice. Clearly a chronological sequence would not be appropriate; there is really no chronology to follow. And presenting his points in order of importance would also be difficult, and would not be persuasive.

Presenting your points in ascending order of importance enables you to build up to the most important item, setting the scene or whetting the person's appetite. Presenting them in descending order makes an impact right at the start, so that you gain your audience's attention. Try numbering the list outline on page 22 in both ascending and descending order of importance and you will see the different effect each method has.

If you are replying to a letter, e-mail or telephone call, it might be best to follow the order in which the other person presented *their* points. Then you can be sure that you have responded to everything. However, this might not be the best way if you are introducing new points not referred to in the original letter or call.

Making your first draft

If you are planning an oral communication, particularly if it is relatively simple, you might stop at this point. However, if you are working on a long presentation it might be better

How would you order the following types of document or conversation?

1 A telephone call replying to a letter of complaint from a client.

2 A report on possible changes to your organisation's internal systems.

3 A sales letter.

4 A letter in response to a request for a quotation.

5 A presentation on the programme for a conference.

to draft out what you are going to say, and if you are planning a written document then it is essential that you do so.

Writing a draft involves organising your points into sentences and paragraphs that flow (see Chapter 4 for more on this), and tightening up your construction and points of grammar. Try to be as precise and to the point as possible, even at this stage; it will make the editing easier later on. Below is an example of a draft letter, based on the list outline shown above, with the points organised in ascending order of importance.

Dear Mr Carter

Thank you for your letter of 12 November enquiring about our fabrics and asking for a quotation. I enclose herewith samples of the different fabrics you asked for, which will give you an idea of the different designs. Each of the designs are unique to our range.

Colour availability is as follows: Design 41 is available in blue and green, Design 53 is available in grey and blue and brown and beige, Design 62 is available in red, and Design 67 is available in black and white and blue and white. Design 18, which you also asked about, is no longer available. It has gone out of fashion and been replaced by more up-to-date designs.

All the designs are the same price, and our price structure is as follows:

Up to 50 metres – £10.00 per metre
50–100 metres – £9.00 per metre
Over 100 metres – £7.50 per metre

For any order over 200 metres, the price is subject to negotiation. Prices include carriage for delivery, and there is an additional 10 per cent off all orders, provided they are received by ourselves before the end of January. Our payment terms are 30 days from date of delivery.

Yours sincerely

There is some work to do, as we shall see in the next section, but it is taking shape the right way.

Editing your draft

Now your document must be 'polished'. You are unlikely to go through this process for any oral communication, otherwise it will sound as though you are reading from a script (which in a sense you will be doing), but for written documents it is essential.

Check your draft to ensure that it says everything that needs saying, but no more, and that it says it as concisely as possible. Editing is quite an art; you can practise your skills on some of the letters, memos, e-mails and reports that *you* receive – can you improve on them?

A Checklist for Editing

- Is your document polite and unemotional?

- Are there any unnecessary words or phrases? If you are not sure try leaving certain phrases out – does this affect the sense of what you are saying?

- How would you react if *you* were receiving it? Is that the reaction you want from your audience?

- Do you assume too much knowledge on the part of your reader?

- Is it clear, or is anything ambiguous?

- If it needs a reply, do you say so? Should you set a time by which you expect to hear from your correspondent?

- Is it likely to achieve the result you want?

- Have you included everything your reader needs to know?

- Have you included anything that is irrelevant to your aim or your audience?

- Is the information logically presented?

- If you are presenting an argument, have you thought of all the counter-arguments?

Below is the final letter based on the draft above. Can you see what has been changed, and why?

MASTERS & CO
Fabric and Furnishings
Masters House, Latherham, YZ23 4WX
Tel. 01456 789012 Fax 014546 901278

19 November 20XX

Mr L. Carter
Bennett & Turner
43 Union Street
Stampton
VW12 3TT

Dear Mr Carter

Thank you for your enquiry of 12 November. I enclose samples of the different fabrics you asked for. Each of the designs shown is unique to our range.

▶

The designs are available in the following colours: Design 41 in blue or green; Design 53 in grey and blue or brown and beige; Design 42 in red only; and Design 67 in black and white or blue and white. I am afraid that Design 18 is no longer available.

All the designs are the same price, and our prices are as follows:

Up to 50 metres – £10.00 per metre
50–100 metres – £9.00 per metre
Over 100 metres – £7.50 per metre.

For orders over 200 metres, the price is subject to negotiation. All these prices include carriage. Our payment terms are 30 days from date of delivery.

We are giving an additional 10 per cent discount on all orders received before the end of January, so if you would like to place an order, why not do so soon and take advantage of this offer?

If you would like further information, please do not hesitate to contact me.

Yours sincerely

Martin Stacey
Sales Executive

- Martin has corrected a few grammatical errors (like 'Each of the designs *is* unique' instead of '*are*') and has changed a few punctuation marks to make the list in the second paragraph easier to follow.
- He has edited out unnecessary words and phrases like 'which will give you an idea of the different designs' in the first paragraph, and 'for delivery' at the end (carriage means delivery).
- He has changed the wording in the first sentence and in the sentence about extra discount, to reduce the number of words in each.
- He has changed the wording and layout of the second paragraph to avoid ambiguity (the way it was expressed in the draft, it was not clear, for example, whether Design 41 was available in both blue and grey, or in a combination of blue and grey).
- He has cut out the explanation for the non-availability of Design 18. It is not really necessary for the customer to know why it has been withdrawn. The explanation as it stands could be interpreted as insulting – suggesting that the customer is out of touch with fashion.
- He has put the sentence about the extra discount at the beginning of a new paragraph to give it more emphasis. He has also made the ending rather more friendly and encouraging.

CHAPTER 3
Laying out documents

The way you lay out any documents you write (including e-mails) can help or hinder your readers' understanding of what you are trying to say. A poorly laid out communication will usually be difficult to follow, but by giving a little thought to its appearance, even if the basic words and structures are the same, you can actually make it easier to read.

Poor layout can also reflect badly on you. Although business communication is becoming more informal, there are still certain right ways of doing things; if you do not follow them, the work will look slipshod and unprofessional to others.

Letters

Letters are perhaps the most important communications to get right because they officially represent your company or organisation to the outside world. Sloppy layout reflects badly not only on you but also on the organisation you represent.

Ordering Your Letter

There can be up to six elements to a business letter, and this is the order in which they should appear:

1. **The date**. This is now almost always shown, in British English, as 23 October 20XX. One still occasionally sees 23rd October 20XX, but that is now much less common. In the USA the month comes before the date – October 23rd 20XX.

2. **Your reference**. It is not essential to include a reference, but it may help you to retrieve a letter from your filing system. It often comprises the initials of the writer and perhaps those of the person who typed the letter, plus a file or account number, for example TRM/HGS/83/4.

3. **Your correspondent's reference**. You should always quote it if they have used one.

4. **The inside address**. This is the name and address of the person to whom the letter is being sent. It is important, because if you do not put it in it will be difficult to remember later who the letter was sent to. It is also so much part of the convention of business letter writing that official letters that do not have an inside address look unprofessional.

5. **The letter itself**.

6. **Any notes about enclosures or copies**. Although it is not essential, it is useful to indicate at the bottom of your letter whether you are enclosing anything with it, and whether any copies are going to other people. The usual abbreviations are:

   – Enc. This means that the recipient should expect to find an enclosure.

   – cc, followed by someone's name. This stands for 'carbon copy' and means that a copy is going to the person named.

   – bcc. This stands for 'blind carbon copy', and is only typed on copies of the letter, also followed by someone's name. It indicates that you are sending a copy to the person named without the original addressee knowing.

Letter layouts

Letters were traditionally laid out in what was called a displayed style, with full punctuation. This meant that the first line of each paragraph was indented, like the paragraphs in a book, and that all punctuation marks were shown, including commas at the end of each line of the inside address and commas after the salutation and complimentary close ('Dear Mr Brown' and 'Yours sincerely'). There were also full stops between the letters of any abbreviations. Below is an example of the start of a letter laid out in this way.

Mr James Baker,
Managing Director,
A.B.C. Cleaning Services,
68 King Street,
Corfield.

Dear Mr Baker,

When you won the contract for the cleaning of our premises, we drew up a very specific schedule of what was required in each building.

As you can see, this looks extremely old-fashioned, and most letters are laid out in what is called the blocked style, with open punctuation. In this format, everything, from the date to the signature, is ranged on the left-hand margin. There is no indenting; new paragraphs are identified by leaving a line space. Punctuation marks are also kept to a minimum. Although they are used in the body of the letter through grammatical necessity, there is no punctuation in the inside address, the salutation or the complimentary close, and no full stops between the letters of abbreviations. Below is a letter laid out in this style.

ROYAL HOTEL
High Street
Lackington
LK1 2JH
Tel. 01567 123456

Our Ref. PLJ/MDR/LG/304
Your Ref. KPS/RMS/4011

6 April 20XX

Mr Keith Sargent
Hamlyn Landscaping
3 Horncaster Lane
Lackington
LK2 4GF

Dear Mr Sargent

Thank you for your letter of 30 March, summarising our discussion regarding the maintenance of our gardens.

We are happy to accept your price but there is just one alteration we would like to make to the agreement you enclosed with your letter. There is no mention of the children's playground, although we did discuss this. As you know, it is a very small area and will not require very much maintenance, but I think it should be specifically mentioned in the agreement, just in case there is some dispute in the future.

Perhaps you could send me an amended contract in due course.

Yours sincerely

Peter Johnson
Manager

cc Jenny Marston, Head Office

Styles of address

It is important to get the name and job title of your correspondent right. If you are replying to a letter, address the person in the form in which he or she has signed. So if someone has signed his letter John Smith, you should address him as John Smith, not J. Smith.

But what do you do if you are replying to a handwritten letter and you cannot decipher the handwriting? The best thing you can do is to make a guess at the name and address and start your letter: 'I hope I have the name and address right. Please excuse me if I have misread your writing.' Do *not* say, 'I could not read your writing.' That will put your reader in the wrong, and start your letter off badly.

There are three ways of addressing a man, and two of addressing a woman. Men can be addressed as:

- James Robinson, Esq.
- Mr James Robinson
- James Robinson

Women can be addressed as:

- Miss (or Mrs or Ms) Susan Brown
- Susan Brown

Esq. (short for Esquire) is very rarely used now, and looks very old fashioned. Even when it was in fairly common use, it was considered very formal. It is, however, still usual to use some form of title (Mr, Mrs, Revd, Dr), although it is becoming more and more common to address people simply as Susan Brown, James Robinson, etc.

So when should you use a title, and when not? There is no hard and fast rule, but generally speaking, if you are writing to a member of the public you should address them as Mr, Mrs, etc. If you are writing to business contacts, it depends to a certain extent on your relationship with them. A title is slightly more formal, and should therefore probably be used for people you have not met. If you have met them, you should be able to judge whether they will be offended if you leave the title out, or whether they are likely to regard you as a bit stuffy if you use it.

It used to be common for women to indicate their marital status with their signature, as in:

Yours sincerely
Margaret James (Mrs).

But most women nowadays, particularly in business, simply sign their names, without indicating their marital status. In this case you should address them as Ms (Ms Susan Brown). This is a generally accepted form of address, although of course if your correspondent has signed herself Mrs or Miss then you should use the same form of address.

Some people can make life difficult for their correspondents by signing with just an initial and a surname – J. Robinson, for example – so that you do not even know what gender they are. The best thing you can do in these circumstances is to make a guess at their gender and address them accordingly. You should then start your letter: 'I hope it is Mr (or Ms) Robinson. Your letter was just signed J. Robinson, so I am not sure.'

Addressing People by Title

If you are writing to an organisation rather than a named individual, you should try to address it to the person who is most likely to deal with your letter: the Sales Manager, the Customer Service Director, the Accountant, etc. If you do not know who might deal with it, here are some tips on who to address it to.

- a company, the Managing Director or the Manager

- a club or a professional institution, the Secretary

- a firm with a sole owner, the Proprietor

- a local authority, the Chief Executive

- a government department in the UK, the Minister or the Permanent Secretary

- a partnership (such as a firm of lawyers or accountants), the Senior Partner. It used to be a rule that they should be addressed as Messrs, as in Messrs Black and Green, but since Messrs is the plural of Mr and the partners are now quite likely to be women, this could give offence.

The salutation

This is the part which opens your letter (which 'salutes' your correspondent), the part that begins 'Dear ...'. If you know your correspondent, there should be no problem deciding on the best salutation. If you know him or her well, you could begin 'Dear John' or 'Dear Mary'. If you do not want to be quite so informal, you could use their title: 'Dear Mr Black' or 'Dear Ms White'. One thing you should *not* do is address someone whose name you know as 'Dear Sir' or 'Dear Madam'. This is so formal and unfriendly as to be almost rude.

A sort of 'halfway house' between these two degrees of formality is becoming increasingly common. It involves using no title in the inside address, and using the person's full name in the salutation. For example, the inside address would be 'Mary White' rather than 'Ms Mary White' and the salutation would be 'Dear Mary White'. The implication is that, although you are not on first-name terms yet, you expect to be fairly soon – perhaps because you are about to develop a business relationship.

If you do not know your correspondent's name, the correct salutation is 'Dear Sir or Madam' (or 'Dear Sir/Madam'). So in all cases where you are addressing someone by their job title only, you should use this form of salutation. You should not assume that the person you are addressing is a man and just write 'Dear Sir', as this could well cause offence if they are a woman. Some people try to get round the formality and clumsiness of 'Dear Sir or Madam' by writing 'Dear Managing Director' or 'Dear Sales Manager', but this has not caught on, and is just as clumsy as 'Dear Sir or Madam'.

Starting your letter

The way you start your letter is important. You should set the tone for the rest of the letter early, and signpost what it is going to be about. You can use a heading if you think it will help clarify the subject immediately; however, headings tend to make letters look rather formal, and they are now used less than they used to be. If you are replying to a letter, then a simple way of indicating the subject is to say: 'Thank you for your letter of 20 March about the trade exhibition.' However, it is important to get a good reaction from your readers, and in order to do so you need to make them want to read on. For this reason, it is best to avoid tired old clichés like 'With reference to your letter of 20 March ...' or 'I am writing to tell you ...' Even 'Thank you for your letter of 20 March' can be avoided with a little thought. Here are a few possible options:

- I was delighted to receive your letter of 20 March about ...
- I was very sorry to see from your letter of 20 March that ...
- Thank you for taking the trouble to write and tell me about ...
- I was concerned to read your letter of 20 March and to see that you have been having problems with ...
- I have thought carefully about the points you raised in your letter of 20 March and ...

There are, of course, many ways of starting your letter, depending on what you are writing about. But do try to make the start both relevant to your subject and interesting, rather than using some of the forms that have been used over and over again. Of course, if you are not replying to a letter, you can get straight into your subject, which makes it easier to avoid clichés. But set the tone as well as the subject from the start. Your reader should be able to tell from your opening not just what the letter is about, but also what you attitude is.

The body of your letter

The main part of your letter should follow on logically from your opening, and there should then be a logical flow through the letter, as discussed in Chapter 2. It should also follow the three rules of business communication and be brief, clear and direct.

Ending your letter

Your closing paragraph is as important as your opening one. This is the last thing your correspondent will read (apart from your signature), and the last impression he or she will be left with. You should use it for three purposes:

- **To summarise your position**. This does not mean that you should provide a summary of everything you have said – that would be boring. You should simply summarise your views, or how you want your reader to feel. The exact wording will depend on the type of letter, but here are a few examples.

  - I hope this has helped you to understand our position.
  - These are the problems I would like to review when we meet.
  - I think you will agree that this is a very special offer.
  - I am sure you will appreciate our concern about this matter.

- **To indicate any action you are expecting, and who will take it**. There are five different forms of action ending, depending on the kind of response you expect. A **positive reader response** means that you expect the reader to take some action. Typical endings of this kind include:

  - I would be grateful if you could let me know as soon as possible what action you intend to take.
  - I look forward to hearing from you.
  - Perhaps you could give me your views on these proposals within the next week or so.
  - Please let me have your cheque in settlement of this account.

A **positive writer response** means that you will be taking some action. For example:

- I will thoroughly investigate the problem and contact you as soon as I have an answer.
- I will consider your proposal carefully and let you have my response within the next few days.
- I am waiting to hear from my accountant and will be in touch as soon as I do.

A **passive reader response** means that the reader has the option of taking some action if he or she wants to, but that you do not expect it. Here are some examples:

- If you need any further information, please let me know.
- If I can be of further assistance, please get in touch .
- If I do not hear from you within the next two weeks, I will assume that you are happy with the new arrangements.

A **passive writer response** means that you might take some action, but that your correspondent should not expect it. Typical endings of this sort might be:

- I will contact you if the situation changes.
- If I receive any further information, I will let you know.

If you do not want to continue the correspondence under any circumstances, then you should make this clear with a **no response** ending. However, do not be rude or abrupt about it; there are polite ways of saying this. Here are some examples which indicate quite clearly that you do not expect to hear from them again:

- Thank you for writing.
- I am grateful for your views.
- I found your comments interesting, and will bear them in mind for the future.

- **To add a courtesy sentence**. If you think it is appropriate, you can include a courtesy sentence. It is not always necessary, but if it suits your aim and your subject, you might want to include something like:
  - Thank you for your co-operation.
  - I apologise for the inconvenience you have been caused.
  - I look forward to a long and profitable business relationship.

  You can, of course, combine a summary, an action ending and a courtesy passage in one sentence. You could, for example, say:
  - These are the problems as I see them, and I would be grateful if you could let me know as soon as possible how you intend to deal with them.
  - I am sure you will understand our concern over the delay in paying, and I look forward to receiving your cheque within the next few days.
  - I apologise for the inconvenience you have been caused, but I hope the arrangements I have made will go some way towards alleviating the problem.

The complimentary close

This is the 'signing off' part of the letter – the part that usually says 'Yours faithfully' or 'Yours sincerely'. In fact these are the only two forms you need to know. However, you do need to know which to use under which circumstances. The rule is quite simple. If your salutation is 'Dear Sir or Madam', then your complimentary close should be 'Yours faithfully'. If your salutation is 'Dear Mr Brown', 'Dear Mrs Green' or 'Dear Robin' then your complimentary close should be 'Yours sincerely'.

You may come across 'Yours truly' in American letters, but it is not used in British business correspondence. Of course, if you are being informal, and writing to someone you know quite well, you can use something like 'With kind regards' or 'With best wishes'.

There should then be a space for the signature, followed by the name of the signatory. If you are writing to someone you know, who knows your position in the organisation, then it is not necessary to include your job title. But if you are writing to a member of the public, or to someone with whom you have not had dealings before, then you should do so, as in:

Ken Stephens
Managing Director.

Sometimes a letter may be dictated by one person but signed by another, usually a secretary or personal assistant (PA). For example, the Marketing Director might dictate a number of letters before going off on a sales trip, and leave them to be typed and signed by her PA. In that case the PA would type the Marketing Director's name and title as usual, but would sign them herself and put a small pp for *per procrationem* (by proxy) before her signature, thus:

Yours sincerely
pp Jane Harrison

Sarah Morgan
Marketing Director

EXERCISE 8

Your company has received a letter from Ashok Kumar, the leader of a local youth club, whom you have not met before, asking for a donation towards the club's activities. As Marketing Manager, you have been asked to reply. Below are some notes outlining what the company has decided. Write a letter based on these notes (they have not necessarily been written down in the most logical order, so you may have to rearrange the points so that your letter flows logically).

- Mr Kumar's letter does not specify what the donation will be used for, and company policy is not to give money without a specific purpose.

- The amount you are prepared to donate will depend on what it is to be used for, so you need a list of the sorts of things the club would like to buy or pay for.

- You are very happy to help local community projects, and the work of the youth club seems to be very worthwhile.

- Because of the nature of your business, you are particularly interested in helping young people appreciate the outdoors.

- If the club runs any outdoor activities you would be happy to contribute towards the cost of equipment or trips.

- Once you have a breakdown of what they are wanting to buy, and approximately how much they think it will cost, you will decide how much you are willing to donate.

Memos and E-mails

Memos

A memo is usually an internal document, sent from one member of an organisation to another. Some organisations have pre-printed memo forms, while others have a house style for the layout of memos. If your organisation does not have a house style, here are a few tips.

The elements of a memo
- the name of the writer

- the name of the addressee

- the date

- the subject

- the body of the memo

You should obviously always indicate who the memo is from, who it is to and the date. These elements should go at the top, but the order in which you put them is up to you. So you might write in any of these forms:

- To: David Cousins
  From: Simon Kitchener
  Date: 22 May 20XX

- From: Simon Kitchener
  To: David Cousins
  Date: 22 May 20XX

- Date: 22 May 20XX
  To David Cousins
  From: Simon Kitchener

You do not have to have a heading in a memo, but it is sometimes a good idea to do so; it tells your reader what the memo is going to be about, and it saves having to explain the subject in the memo itself. So you memo might read:

To: David Cousins
From: Simon Kitchener
Date: 22 May 20XX

ARRANGEMENTS FOR GRADUATE INTERVIEWS

This tells your reader immediately what to expect. It also saves you having to include a sentence such as 'I would like to discuss this year's arrangements for graduate interviews.' This might provide all the introduction you need, but you might also want to write a short introductory paragraph as well, giving some of the background.

The main part of the memo should be laid out in a logical sequence, as described in Chapter 2, and should be followed by a final paragraph, which might serve a variety of purposes, depending on the subject: it might indicate any action to be taken, present any recommendations or conclusions, or summarise your arguments.

Although most memos, being internal communications between colleagues, may be expressed in slightly less formal language than letters, they should still conform to the requirements of all business communications and be brief, clear and direct.

E-mails

In most organisations memos have been replaced by e-mails as the main written form of internal communication, but the same rules generally apply. Of course, the first three elements – writer's name, addressee's name and the date – are all inserted automatically, and you will be prompted to insert a subject. The body of the e-mail, however, should be written in the same way as a memo. In personal e-mails it is common not to worry too much about spelling, capital letters or punctuation, to use abbreviations (and sometimes even mobile phone text language), and to include 'emoticons', but these have no place in business e-mails. You should be using correct, clear English. And if you are e-mailing someone outside your organisation, then the format should be the same as for letters (apart from the inside address), including the correct salutation and complimentary close.

Reports

Reports can serve a wide variety of purposes, and therefore have a number of different formats. Most, however, follow the same basic pattern, regardless of the subject or aim. This pattern is:

- the preliminary pages
- the introduction
- the body of the report
- the conclusion, recommendation or main findings

These sections are found in almost all reports. In addition, there may be two more sections at the end:

- acknowledgements
- appendices

Types of Report

There are three main categories of report, each with a slight variation on the basic pattern.

- **Recommendation reports**, as their name suggests, are written with the aim of recommending some sort of action. They may include a conclusion or conclusions as well, but they need not always do so.

- **Conclusion reports** are similar in that they probably present different arguments for and against a course of action. The difference is that they do not make recommendations. A feasibility study is an example of this kind of report. You might be asked to look into the feasibility of a certain course of action; you would reach a conclusion as to whether it was a viable proposition or not, but you would not make any recommendation.

- **Information reports** only present information. You might brief someone or provide background information, and you would probably present your main findings, but because of the nature of this kind of report, it would contain no conclusion or recommendation.

Preliminary pages

Before you start your actual report, you need to provide certain information. Your preliminary pages would include:

- The title page. This should give the title of the report, who it is by, the date it was written and the distribution. A typical title page might look like this:

MANAGEMENT STRUCTURES
AT GUNTON ENGINEERING LTD

By
Yvonne Macdonald
24 November 20XX

To: All directors and managers

- **A summary.** This is not necessary for a short report, but if it is a long one, it is a good idea to provide a brief summary (no more than 150 words), giving the gist of what the report contains, and the main conclusions, recommendations or findings. This helps busy executives, who may not need to work through the whole report, to see at a glance what it is about. It should be on a page by itself, headed 'Summary'. Below is an example of such a summary.

SUMMARY

The current management structure at Gunton's is hierarchical, with a great deal of direction from above.

There is strong evidence that this causes resentment in the junior grades. There is also evidence to suggest that the structure leads to 'empire building'. Both these factors appear to have a deadening effect on initiative and creativity.

A more flexible structure would alleviate these problems, but it would require a complete revision of responsibilities and would cause disruption in the short term. It would, moreover, require a complete change in management style and attitude, from the top down.

However, if the changes were well planned and handled sympathetically, the disruption could be kept to a minimum, and they would undoubtedly result in greater efficiency and improved morale.

If the company is to meet the challenges of the future and remain competitive, I believe it is essential that the changes are made.

- **A table of contents.** Again, this is only necessary if the report is long. It should also be on a page by itself. In it you can list the major headings and the pages on which they appear.

The introduction

In this section you give the background to the report itself: why it was written, what it is about, who it is intended for, who asked for it, and the investigative and other methods used. But be careful to give *only* the background to your report in the introduction – there can be a temptation to let the introduction merge into the body of the report, which will only cause confusion.

Writing Your Introduction

Use the following checklist to ensure that your introduction contains all the information it should, but nothing else.

- Is it clear why the report was written?

- Do you say who it was written for?

- Does it give an idea of the subject of the report *without* giving details of the actual investigation or the conclusions, recommendations or main findings?

Below is an example of the introduction to a report.

INTRODUCTION

I was asked by the Managing Director to investigate the management structures at Gunton's Engineering Ltd, to find out whether they are still appropriate in view of recent developments within the company and in the business environment, and to make recommendations for any changes I thought were necessary.

This report, which is intended as a discussion document for all directors and managers, is the result of my investigation. I was asked particularly to address it to managers as well as directors, as it was felt that my conclusions should be seen and discussed by everyone who might be affected by them.

I looked carefully at the present structure, how it was established and how it has evolved. Over a period of four weeks, I watched management in action by attending meetings, including Board meetings, and by sitting in on formal and informal one-to-one and group discussions between managers and directors.

I then discussed with every manager and director his or her views on the structure, and what he or she saw as its strengths and weaknesses. I also canvassed their views on alternative models, and how they might apply to Gunton's. I obtained the opinions of non-management staff through the Staff Council and trade union representatives.

My conclusions and recommendations are based on my assessment of the present structure and how it affects all aspects of the company's performance, together with my assessment of the attitudes of the managers, directors and other staff, and of the alternative models that might be applied.

The body of the report

This is obviously the largest part, as it is where you set out all the relevant information: what you have discovered during your investigation, the facts on which you base any arguments, conclusions or recommendations, the details you have been asked to provide.

Obviously your report should flow logically, as outlined in Chapter 2. The particular pattern you adopt will depend on the nature of the report. An analytical report should usually develop a logical argument, building up to a conclusion and/or recommendations, whereas a briefing report would probably have the sections set out in order of priority. But there might be reports that are better laid out in chronological order. Reports can also be sectionalised, each section dealing with a different department or field of activity, but each section will still need to follow one of the above patterns. So, as indicated in Chapter 2, it is vital that you order your points in a logical sequence.

How you actually set out your report depends on how long it is, and what it is to be used for. Here are a few tips.

- If it is a long report, you should use headed sections. Start each new section on a new page, like the chapters in a book. This looks better, and is easier to absorb, than a long mass of text.
- If it is not long enough to sectionalise in this way, you should still consider using headings within the text.
- If it is fairly complex, you might use different weights of heading, rather like the headings in this book – say block capitals for main headings, bold for subheadings, italic for sub-subheadings.

- If people are likely to want to refer to specific paragraphs, or if you need to cross-refer from one paragraph to another, then you might number the paragraphs. Your headings could be numbered 1, 2, 3, etc., and if there are subsections they could be numbered 1.1, 1.2, 1.3, etc. Any sub-subsections would then be numbered 1.1.1, 1.1.2, 1.1.3, etc. Alternatively, you could use (a), (b), (c) for subsections and (i), (ii), (iii) for sub-subsections. Below is a section of a report laid out in this way.

3. THE CONDUCT OF MEETINGS

The way in which meetings are conducted at Gunton's varies considerably, depending on their composition. I have classified the meetings into three groups, each of which has a different composition, and each of which is therefore conducted in a different way.

(a) Peer Group Meetings

These are meetings between people at roughly the same level in the organisation: directors with directors, senior managers with senior managers, junior managers with junior managers, supervisors with supervisors.

(i) Discussion at these meetings is usually vigorous, with a high level of participation. Participants are not generally apprehensive about expressing their views (but see Paragraph (ii) below), and conclusions are reached after all sides of the argument have been heard.

(ii) It is noticeable, however, that the lower down the scale of seniority the participants are, the more restricted their deliberations become. Discussion is still vigorous, but it does not necessarily cover all aspects of the subject. A meeting of junior managers, for example, discussed at length how they might improve communications at their level. At a certain point, it became obvious that policy aspects were involved; at that point the discussion veered away, as if the participants were by mutual agreement avoiding giving their opinions on matters that were outside their own narrow areas of responsibility.

The conclusion, recommendations or main findings

Some people prefer to put this section at the beginning of their report, immediately after the introduction, so that readers can see what they have concluded and then read the background information on which the recommendation or conclusion is based. I do not recommend this order, however, particularly if you think some of your readers might resist your conclusions. If they see and disagree with your conclusions before reading the facts on which they are based, they may well look at the facts with a jaundiced eye, trying to pick holes in your arguments. It is better, and more logical, for them to look at the facts first. That, after all, is how you yourself will have reached your conclusion, so that is the way to lead your readers to the same conclusion.

If this section consists of your main findings or highlights from the report rather than a conclusion – in other words, if it is something like a briefing report, which does not present an argument – then there is perhaps not the same need to put it at the end. However, I would still prefer to see it there. If your main findings appear at the beginning, your readers will be tempted to read only them, and to skip the rest. But if your report has been written properly, there should be nothing in it that is not necessary, so those readers who skip the body of the report will miss some important information. Moreover, a section of highlights at the end serves as a useful summation and reminder of what has gone before.

In an investigative or analytical report, you may discover several possible solutions to the problem you have been investigating. You may, of course, only *recommend* one solution, but you should give all the possibilities in your conclusion, with their advantages and disadvantages. If your report is to contain both a conclusion and a recommendation, then put them in two separate sections. It only makes the report confusing if you try to combine both a conclusion and a recommendation in one section.

Your recommendation should follow on logically from the facts and arguments you have presented earlier in your report. Always give your reasons for recommending a particular course of action, especially if you have proposed several possible solutions in your conclusion and are recommending just one. If you are making more than one recommendation they should be numbered, to make them clearer and easier to differentiate.

Be very specific in your recommendations. It is no good saying, 'I recommend that the management structure of Gunton's be changed', or even 'I recommend that the management structure of Gunton's be made more flexible, with greater responsibility for junior managers.' What exactly does this mean? Say more specifically *what* the new structure should be and *how* it should be brought in. Or, at the very least, recommend that the structure be changed and that a working party be set up (specifying its composition and terms of reference) to see how best to introduce it. You might also suggest a timescale for introducing the measures recommended. Your report is less likely to be politely ignored or shelved if you make your recommendation specific and give a timescale.

Acknowledgements

Most reports will not need an acknowledgements section, but if you use material from other sources you should acknowledge it. Do not try to pass someone else's work off as your own. Not only is this dishonest, but if you are found out, it will discredit everything you have written, even the parts that *are* your own work.

But you do not want to clutter up the body of the report with acknowledgements; they will interrupt the flow of your argument. So if you do need to acknowledge the help of other people, or if you have referred to their written work, you will need a separate acknowledgements section. How you lay it out is largely a matter of personal preference. If you just want to thank certain people for their help, then you can simply say, 'I would like to acknowledge the help of the following people in the compilation of this report:' and then list their names. Alternatively you can actually mention what help they gave you. If, on the other hand, you have referred to documents and publications, then it is customary to give full publication information. There is no 'right' way of presenting it, so long as everything is there that a reader would need if they wanted to refer to the publications themselves. Look at the acknowledgements sections of other people's reports, and at the bibliographies of books, and choose a system that you like. But once you have chosen a system, stick to it and be consistent throughout this section.

If you actually quote from an article or book in your report, then you should acknowledge the quote in the text, giving the page reference. So you might put in brackets after a quote: (Smith, p. 27). The reader can then refer to your acknowledgements section to find the publication you are quoting from.

Acknowledging Publications Referred To

It is customary, when acknowledging publications, to give the following information:

- In the case of books, the author, the title, the publisher, and usually the year of publication (shown in the copyright information of the book), e.g. Smith, P.J. *Business Organisation*, Jones & Co., 20XX.

- In the case of journal or magazine articles, the author, the titles of the article and the publication, the volume and number (or date) of the particular issue, and usually the year of publication, e.g. Smith, P.J. 'Organising an Accounting System', *Small Trader*, Vol. 7, No. 12, 20XX.

- In the case of government documents, the department or author, the title, the document number if there is one, the publisher if it is a published document, and the year of issue, e.g. Department for Universities, Skills and Enterprise. *Training Employees on the Job*, Cmnd 6354, HMSO, 20XX.

- In the case of unpublished documents, the author, the title, what the document is and the year of issue, e.g. Smith, P.J. *Organisational Dynamics in Multinational Organisations*, PhD thesis, University of Liverpool, 20XX.

Appendices

The body of your report should be as short and as interesting as possible, without omitting anything important, so as to keep your readers' attention. However, there will be times when you need to provide long documents or tables of figures to support your arguments. These will only clutter up the report and, like acknowledgements, spoil the flow of your argument. If you feel they are necessary, therefore, it is a good idea to mention just the main features in the report itself, but to reproduce the whole document as an appendix. For example, you might say: 'You may recall that in his report on the new computer systems last year, Jeremy Cornwood concluded that some systems would be better organised on a product rather than a departmental basis (see Appendix A).' You would then reproduce the whole of Jeremy Cornwood's report as Appendix A.

The same principle applies even when you are referring not to a previously issued document, but to something you have prepared yourself. For example: 'A department-by-department analysis of the company's overheads in the last five years shows a worrying increase in the Systems Department's share in relation to other departments (see Appendix B).' You would then attach your analysis of overheads as Appendix B.

EXERCISE 9

A new Chief Executive has recently taken over at your company or organisation. Write a report briefing him or her on what your department does and how it operates. If you do not work for an organisation at present, then write about any organisation of which you are a member – a club, college, school, voluntary organisation, etc.

Incorporating Tables and Charts

No matter how good your command of English, no matter how good you are at writing, there are times when words and figures are not enough. There are times when, to make what you want to say quite clear, you need a more visual approach. That is when tables and charts come into their own.

When planning to use these devices, however, you will need to choose the right format – the wrong choice will make the information more confused, not less. You should also carefully plan your layout and how you intend to use your space. Are you going to put tables and charts in an appendix or in the text of your report? Both have their advantages and disadvantages.

- Putting charts in the text is a bit more complicated, as you have to import them into your document. You also need to be sure that all your readers will want all the information they contain; if some do not, you might be better to mention the main points illustrated by the chart in the text and put the chart itself in an appendix.
- If all your readers are likely to be interested in your charts, it will be more convenient if they can refer to them while reading your report, which will be easier if they are in the text, even though it might be more complicated for you.

Of course, if you are using tables or charts in a presentation, then they will appear as separate slides anyway.

Tables

It is not the purpose of this book to show you how to calculate the figures, percentages, averages, etc. you may need in your documents or presentations, just to show you some of the ways in which they can be presented.

The easiest, and perhaps the most common, way to show figures is to tabulate them. How you present your tables will depend on the information you want to highlight. As an example, let us consider how you might present a comparison between two years' sales figures, broken down into sales areas. At its simplest, such a table might look like this:

	Year 1 Sales Value	Year 2 Sales Value
UK	£250,000	£270,000
EU	£100,000	£110,000
Rest of Europe	£30,000	£30,000
USA	£70,000	£70,000
Asia	£30,000	£40,000
Rest of the World	£20,000	£22,000
TOTAL	£500,000	£542,000

This is fine, if that is all the information you want to show. Your audience can see immediately that UK sales increased by £20,000, while Asian sales increased by £10,000. But what if you want to say something about the relative effectiveness of your sales efforts in the two markets? Your audience can probably work out that Asia's £10,000 increase is better than the UK's £20,000. But your job is to make your point easy to understand: if you want them to make that kind of comparison, you should present your figures in a way that enables them to do so easily. You could, for example, simply add a column to each of the years, showing each area's sales as a percentage of the total – what is called the profile.

	Year 1		Year 2	
	Sales Value	Profile %	Sales Value	Profile %
UK	£250,000	50	£270,000	49.8
EU	£100,000	20	£110,000	20.3
Rest of Europe	£30,000	6	£30,000	5.5
USA	£70,000	14	£70,000	12.9
Asia	£30,000	6	£40,000	7.4
Rest of World	£20,000	4	£22,000	4.1
TOTAL	£500,000	100	£542,000	100

Now you can see that UK sales as a proportion of the total actually fell, from 50 to 49.8 %, despite the actual rise in sales, and that Asia's increased, from 6 to 7.4%. This could be vital information when planning further strategies.

Again, that is fine, if that is the picture you want to convey. But sometimes you may want not only to compare actual figures, but also perhaps to see how much each segment has contributed to the increase or decrease. Using the figures above, you know that the UK's sales have increased by £20,000. You also know that total sales have increased by £42,000. But suppose you wanted to compare the UK's share of *that increase* (its profile of the increase), with that, say of the EU. This is done by adding three more columns, as shown below.

	Year 1		Year 2				
	Sales Value	Prof %	Sales Value	Prof %	Increase	Inc %	Inc Prof %
UK	£250,000	50	£270,000	49.8	£20,000	8	47.6
EU	£100,000	20	£110,000	20.3	£10,000	10	23.8
Rest of Europe	£30,000	6	£30,000	5.5	–	–	–
USA	£70,000	14	£70,000	12.9	–	–	–
Asia	£30,000	6	£40,000	7.4	£10,000	33.3	23.8
Rest of World	£20,000	4	£22,000	4.1	£2,000	10	4.8
TOTAL	£500,000	100	£542,000	100	£42,000		100

Two notes of warning should be sounded at this stage. First, tables should *simplify* your document. Only include information that is relevant; do not bore your audience with long tables of figures, only some of which have a bearing on what you are trying to communicate. You would be foolish to use the above table, for example, unless you really did need to convey the profile of the increase of each area.

Second, make sure that you quote *all* the relevant figures; do not use just the ones that prove your point. As Disraeli once said, there are 'lies, damned lies and statistics', and there is no doubt that statistics can be, and often are, used to distort and confuse the facts. Using the above figures, for example, if your agent in Asia asked for an increase in commission, would you argue that he does not deserve it because he has only increased his share of the total market from 6 to 7.4%? Or that he contributed only 23.8% to the year's increase in sales? Superficially, these might seem like good arguments based on sound statistics. But he has been working from a lower base than other agents, so you could not expect him to have contributed as much to the overall increase. He would be quite justified in pointing out that he has increased sales in his area by 33% – over three times as much as anyone else.

If your figures include averages, make sure that the averages make sense. Do not let unusual items distort them. For example, your company's expenditure in six successive months might be as follows:

January	£40,000
February	£36,000
March	£130,000
April	£38,500
May	£34,500
June	£36,250
Average	£52,541

This average bears no relation to any of the monthly figures. It is much higher than most of them, and much lower than March's. March was an aberration. Perhaps you bought some new machinery, which cost £95,000. It would make more sense then to take that extraordinary, one-off expenditure out of the average calculation, and to note it separately, as follows:

January	£40,000
February	£36,000
March	£35,000
April	£38,500
May	£34,500
June	£36,250
Average	£36,708

Note: In March there was a further payment of £95,000 for new machinery, which is not shown in these figures.

Graphs

There are times when raw information, even in the form of a table, does not make enough of an impact. Since your aim is to make your audience's job easier, you need a way of presenting difficult information in an easily digestible form. Sometimes that form needs to be visual, and one of the common forms of visual presentation is the graph.

Graphs are used for a variety of purposes, but the most common in business is to show a trend over time. The cost of salaries, sales figures, production costs, number of employees, goods produced and overheads are just some of the many statistics that can be plotted graphically to show the underlying trend. To illustrate this, let us assume that you are a manufacturer. You are taking a long-term look at the costs of your raw materials. Over a six-year period, the cost per item produced is as follows:

Year 1: £6.00

Year 2: £6.42

Year 3: £7.00

Year 4: £6.90

Year 5: £7.90

Year 6: £8.54

A graph of these figures would look like this:

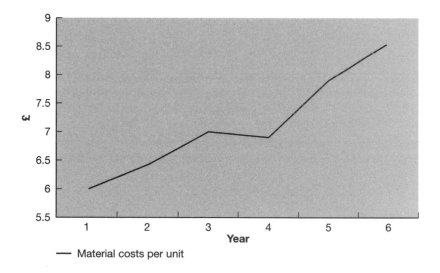

— Material costs per unit

This illustrates that, apart from a dip in Year 4, your raw material costs have shown a fairly steady rise. The figures themselves, of course, would show that costs were rising, but the graph brings home how steady the rise is, and what an aberration the Year 4 figure is. It might prompt you to investigate the reason for the dip.

You can also compare different sets of figures by plotting two or more lines on the same graph – overheads for different departments, for example. You can even compare trends in different fields by using a device called indexing. This enables you to compare a trend in, say, overheads (which are expressed in thousands of pounds) with something like the number of employees (expressed as a quantity). It involves giving your first year's figure, whether it is a monetary value, a quantity or a percentage, a value of 100, and relating all subsequent figures to it in proportion. For example, the figures which made up the above graph, expressed as an index, would be:

Year 1: 100

Year 2: 107 (£6.42 is 1.07 times £6.00)

Year 3: 117 (£7.00 is 1.17 times £6.00)

Year 4: 115

Year 5: 132

Year 6: 142

The value of indexing can be seen if you want to compare your costs with, say, the rate of inflation. This is a percentage, but it can still be plotted on the same graph. The figures might be:

Year 1: 5% (index 100)

Year 2: 6% (106)

Year 3: 7% (113)

Year 4: 6% (120)

Year 5: 7% (128)

Year 6: 6% (137)

The comparison in trends can be seen by changing the vertical axis of the above graph to show index figures, not monetary values, and adding another line, as below.

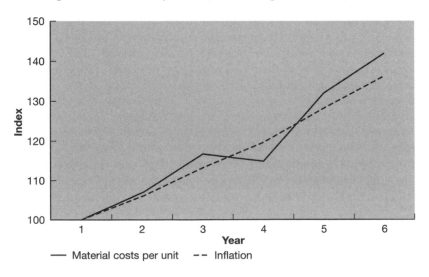

This shows a more disturbing picture, namely that material costs are rising at a higher rate than the rate of inflation. It is therefore a trend that might need watching.

You do not have to use indexing, of course. If all the items you want to plot can be expressed in the same terms, you can plot actual values. But you need to ensure that you are comparing like with like. It would not be very helpful, for example, to plot costs and prices without indexing, even though both are monetary values. In the first place, prices are likely to be so much higher than costs that a slight fluctuation in prices will look very much bigger than a similar fluctuation in costs. In the graph below, for example, the upward trend in prices looks very much steeper than the trend in costs, because the values are so much higher. In fact the percentage rise is much lower, as you can see by comparing this graph with the next one, which uses indexing. Another problem with trying to plot such widely different values is that you end up with a very long vertical axis, with a line at the bottom for costs and a line at the top for prices, which does not help anyone's understanding.

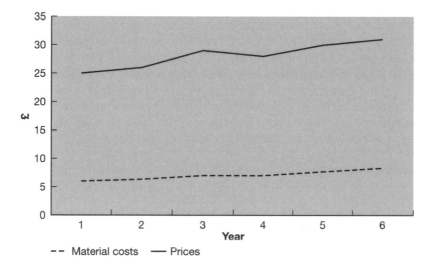

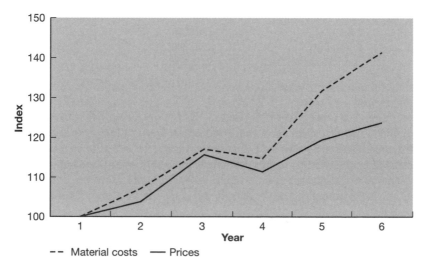

When plotting a graph on your computer, you will be prompted to label the axes, but if you are doing it by hand you need to remember to do so clearly, as your audience might otherwise be confused. You should also show the gradations clearly. If you are doing it on your computer, it will automatically start the axes at 0, but this might not be the best format (the graphs above, for example, would not be nearly as clear if the vertical axis started at 0). So you may need to format the scales. If one axis stands for time, it should always be the horizontal one.

You can add as many lines to your graph as you like, but do not clutter it, or it will become difficult to interpret. It is best to differentiate the lines with different colours, but if that is not possible, or if the graph will need to be photocopied in black and white, then show them as solid and broken lines. You can also mark the lines at the precise points where you plotted the different values, so that your audience can see those values in each year.

Bar charts

Graphs are very good for showing trends, but not so good if you want to compare two types of data at a particular time. You can, of course, do this by comparing the points on the graph, but the comparative values are not easily apparent – and as always your aim should be to make your audience's task easier. This is where a bar chart comes into its own. You can show a particular year's (or month's, or country's, or product group's) figures for a number of different departments (or activities, or product lines, or countries, or anything else) and have an instant comparison. If you show the figures for more than one period, it will also show you the trend, but not as clearly as a graph.

Here are some statistics showing the overheads of the various departments of a wholesaler.

Year 1:	Sales:	£250,000
	Distribution	£168,500
	Accounts and Systems	£253,200
Year 2:	Sales:	£307,000
	Distribution	£177,000
	Accounts and Systems	£267,500
Year 3:	Sales:	£362,500
	Distribution	£187,500
	Accounts and Systems	£279,000

A bar chart of these figures would look like the first chart on page 51:

As you can see, it is easy to pick out that in Year 1 the Sales Department's overheads were one and a half times those of the Distribution Department and about the same as those of Accounts and Systems. It is also very easy to see that in Year 3 they were almost double those for Distribution and much higher than those for Accounts and Systems. This is much clearer in a bar chart than in a table or graph. Note that it is customary to show the actual figures as well as the scale, as it can be difficult to read across from the scale.

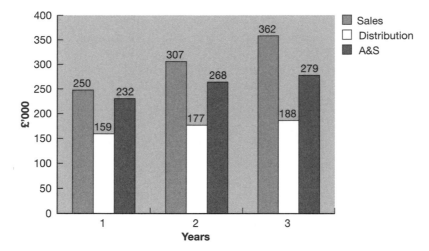

You can make bar charts more sophisticated by subdividing the bars. So, for example, you could subdivide each department's bar, using different colours or shading for different overhead categories, as shown below. This will show your audience why the Sales Department's overheads have increased by so much more than those of the other departments.

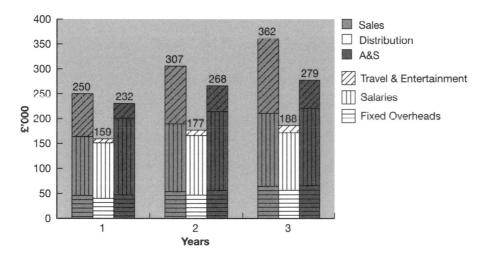

Pie charts

Pie charts are a good way of showing in what proportions a total figure is split between various subdivisions. The wholesaler's figures for Year 1, for example, could be presented in this way, as shown on page 52.

Indeed, this would be the best way of presenting them if the aim was to show how the company's overheads were divided between the three departments. But it is not a good way of making comparisons between one set of figures and another. The pie chart shows more clearly than the bar chart what share of the company's total overheads is allocated to each department, but it is not so easy to see that the Sales Department's overheads are one and half times those of Distribution.

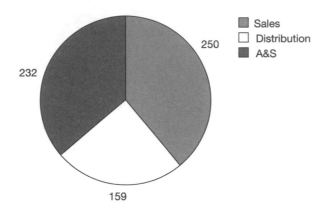

Pie charts can be used for all sorts of figures when you want to show the segmentation of a total – for example sales figures split into sales areas, total turnover divided into different product lines, or expenditure shown by cost centre. But it is inadvisable to have more than seven segments, otherwise some of them become so small that they lose their impact. As with bar charts, it is usual to show the actual figures for each segment.

EXERCISE 10

Which type of visual display would you use to illustrate the following:

1. the contribution each of a number of product lines has made to a company's overall increase in profits over a period of three years

2. how a local authority's revenue is divided between different services

3. how the turnover of three different branches of a business compare, and how the relative figures have changed over four years

4. how the turnover of a company has risen over five years, in comparison with the number of people it employs

Flow charts

Flow charts are not used to present figures, but rather to show the flow of work or activity diagrammatically. As always, the aim is to make it easier for your audience to understand what you are saying, and very often a flow chart does this better than a verbal description. Below is a simple flow chart for an office dealing with customer enquiries and using standard letters. As you can see, by following the arrows and instructions it is easy to see what needs to be done at each stage.

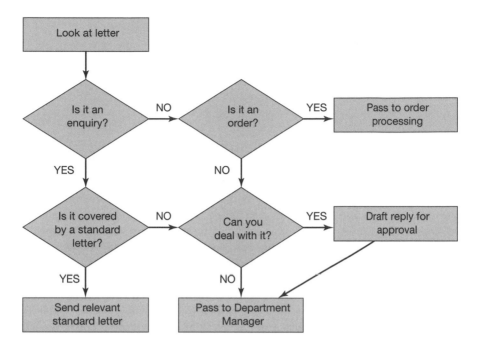

Conventions in Using Flow Charts

- The flow should always go from top to bottom and from left to right.

- You should clearly label each activity or decision.

- Use different kinds of box to indicate decisions and actions. In the example shown, actions are represented by rectangles and decisions by lozenges.

- Each step should be shown in its logical order in the process.

- Use arrows to indicate the direction of 'flow'.

CHAPTER 4

Constructing sentences and paragraphs

In any document, it is important to get your construction right. When you are planning an oral report or presentation, the actual sentence and paragraph construction may not be as important, but even then the overall shape needs some thought, because that is what dictates the structure of what you are going to say: where you are going to pause, how you are going to divide your subject into easily absorbed segments, etc. No matter how interesting you try to make your subject, no matter how logical your argument is, people will find it difficult to follow if it is not well put together.

The basic building blocks of your communication are the words you use; these are built up to form sentences, which in turn are built up to make paragraphs. Here we are concerned with the way you put words together – the sentences you use and how you put them together to form paragraphs.

What Is a Sentence?

We all think we know what a sentence is – after all, we use them thousands of times a day. But are we quite sure that the sentences we use are real sentences?

A sentence is defined as 'a set of words complete in itself, containing a subject and a predicate'. There are two terms here that need a bit of explaining. The subject is the person or thing the sentence is about; it must be a noun, a pronoun or a noun clause, but not a relative pronoun. (If you do not understand these parts of speech, see Chapter 7.) So you cannot say, 'I have received your letter. Which points out an error in your account.' The second part of the passage is not a sentence, because there is no subject. The word 'which' is a relative pronoun, which introduces a description of the letter. The passage should read, 'I have received your letter, which points out an error in your account.'

The predicate tells you something about the subject, and must contain a verb. The predicate can describe the subject or say what it did or was, or what was done to it. Here are a few examples.

- **I apologise for the delay**. Here the subject is 'I' (that is who the sentence is about). The predicate is 'apologise for the delay' (that tells us something about the subject – what I am doing.
- **The cheque is in the post**. Here the subject is 'The cheque' and the predicate is 'is in the post' (it describes the cheque).
- **The meeting adjourned**. This is an instance where the predicate contains *only* a verb – 'adjourned' tells us what the meeting (the subject) did.

A common grammatical mistake in business communication is to write 'non-sentences' – passages that are used as sentences but do not contain both a subject and a predicate. This is not necessarily crucial when you are speaking, as the rules do not have to be applied quite so rigorously, but in correspondence it looks sloppy. So you should not say, 'Hoping this meets with your approval.' This is not a sentence; it has no subject. Who is hoping? You should say, 'I hope this meets with your approval.' Now there is a subject – 'I'. It is also wrong to say, 'There is only one problem. The cost.' 'The cost' is not a sentence, as it has no predicate. This passage should read, 'There is only one problem: the cost.'

There are two instances when it is permissible to use what look like 'non-sentences': the expression 'thank you', which is short for 'I thank you'; and requests, invitations or demands, like 'Please let me know if I can help you.'

Types of Sentence

There are four types of sentence, distinguished by their complexity.

- A **simple sentence** has only one predicate, although it can have more than one subject. It is usually short. For example:
  - I have received your letter.
  - You and I must meet next week.

- A **compound sentence** consists of two or more simple sentences joined by a conjunction. For example:
  - I have received your letter and I agree with what you say.
  - You and I must meet next week, but I am out of the office on Tuesday and I am involved in meetings all day on Wednesday.

- A **complex sentence** consists of a main clause and one or more subordinate clauses (for an explanation of clauses, see Chapter 7). For example:
  - I have received your letter, which sets out your views very clearly.
  - You and I must meet next week, because we need to make arrangements for the Sales Clerk interviews.

- A **compound complex sentence** has two or more main clauses as well as subordinate ones. For example:
  - I have received your letter, which sets out your views very clearly, and the Manager, to whom I showed it, agrees with what you say.
  - You and I must meet next week, because we need to make arrangements for the Sales Clerk interviews, but I am out of the office on Tuesday, which could be a problem.

A sentence should normally convey a single idea. It can sometimes contain two ideas which are closely connected, but there should never be more than that. If it does contain two ideas, then they must be joined by a conjunction or a relative pronoun (if you do not know what these are, see Chapter 7), or by a semicolon (see Chapter 8). A very common mistake is to write something like this: 'I enclose your latest statement, I would like to point out that there is an amount of £270 outstanding.' This sentence contains two ideas: the statement and the amount outstanding. They are probably close enough to be included in the same sentence, but they are not joined by a conjunction, a relative pronoun or a semicolon. The comma does not provide enough of a pause between the two ideas, and the sentence looks wrong (and would probably sound wrong if read). It should be one of the following:

- I enclose your latest statement, and would like to point out that there is an amount of £270 outstanding.
- I enclose you latest statement, which I would like to point out shows an amount of £270 outstanding.
- I enclose your latest statement; I would like to point out that there is an amount of £270 outstanding.

Loose and periodic sentences

There are two types of sentence construction: loose and periodic.

- A **loose sentence** has the subject first, as in: 'I will circulate a paper before the meeting.'
- A **periodic sentence** puts subsidiary phrases or clauses before the subject, as in: 'Before the meeting, I will circulate a paper.'

As you can see from these examples, loose sentences are more direct, and since one of the rules of business communication is to be direct, they are to be preferred. However, periodic sentences can be useful for building up to your subject, conveying a sense almost of suspense. They are therefore good for sales letters, where your aim is to hold the reader's attention and make them want to know what is coming next. Look at the following extract.

```
Welcome to our brand new, exciting autumn catalogue. As you browse through it, you will, I
am sure, be delighted by the superb range of furniture we now offer. Whether you are looking
for something traditional or ultra-modern, you will find it here. We have furniture for
every room in the house, from beds to armchairs, dining tables to desks, all from the top
manufacturers, and all at very attractive prices. Indeed, for value for money, you will find
our terms hard to beat.
```

Can you see how periodic sentences are used in this way? 'As you browse through it', 'Whether you are looking for something traditional or ultra-modern', 'Indeed, for value for money' are all used to keep people reading, to whet their appetite.

Periodic sentences are also useful to make a connection between two sentences, to refer back from one to the other. Look at the following two passages:

- Can we meet soon? Before the meeting I will circulate a paper.
- Can we meet soon? I will circulate a paper before the meeting.

The first is better than the second, because 'before the meeting' connects the two sentences by referring back to the first.

Sentence length

How long should your sentences be? The answer is 'as long as necessary, but no longer'. This may not seem very helpful, but it is true – there is no 'best' length. It all depends on the circumstances. Short sentences generally give a sense of rapid movement and tension, a feeling of urgency. Longer ones are often used in descriptive passages, to develop your argument or perhaps to provide background information. They can give an impression of having been well thought out, and so are good to use from time to time in a report, for example.

Because your aim is to be direct and brief, you should generally *prefer* short sentences. This is especially true when speaking, because if your sentences become too long you may well find it difficult yourself to keep track of what you are saying, let alone your audience! But do not feel that you must always use them. Apart from the fact that there are times when longer sentences are more in keeping with what you want to convey, it is also good to have a mixture of sentence lengths to avoid monotony and the 'scrappy' appearance of too many short, simple sentences. It can sometimes be harder for your audience to absorb a number of different simple sentences, all with what appear to be unconnected bits of information, than to make sense of one longer one. Look at the following passage from an e-mail.

We must operate as efficiently as possible. I have therefore asked all staff for their ideas on ways to do this. Here are some of their ideas.

We could send all mail by second-class post. This would save us several thousand pounds. It would also make our service worse. We would have to weigh the saving against the loss of customer goodwill.

We could introduce more flexible working practices. Staff could be trained to do several jobs. This would mean that they could be switched to different activities if necessary. For example, the order input clerks might be overloaded. In that case some of the accounts clerks could be moved across to help them.

As you can see, using just short, simple sentences makes the document disjointed, and the reader finds it difficult to follow the flow of the argument.

Now look at the following.

Because it is important that we operate as efficiently as possible, I have asked all staff for their ideas on ways to do this. Here are some of those ideas.

We could send all mail by second-class post, which would save us several thousand pounds. However, we would have to weigh the saving against the loss of customer goodwill caused by the worsening of service that would result.

We could introduce more flexible working practices. Staff could be trained to do several jobs, so that they could be switched to different activities if necessary. For example, if the order input clerks were overloaded, some of the accounts clerks could be moved across to help them.

This is very much easier to read because there is a mixture of sentence types and lengths, and the document flows more fluidly because closely connected subjects are linked.

As we have seen, a sentence should convey a single idea or two related ideas, and it should therefore be as long as is necessary to convey that idea, or those ideas, but no longer. Look at the following sentence: 'The customer's complaint, which concerned the poor quality of our products, should have been dealt with immediately.' It is not particularly long, but it is awkward, because it contains two ideas: the nature of the complaint and the fact that it should have been dealt with immediately. These ideas are not close enough to justify being in the same sentence, so it should have been written: 'The customer's complaint concerned the poor quality of our products. It should have been dealt with immediately.' If the subsidiary clause had been 'which was received a week ago' then it would have been acceptable to have just one sentence, as the idea that it was received a week ago is linked to the idea that it should have been dealt with immediately.

On the other hand, you can have some quite long sentences that are acceptable, since they convey just one idea; it all depends on the idea. For example, the following sentence has one idea, and it is short: 'If we promote John Smith, he might not be able to cope with the extra responsibility.' The idea is that John Smith might not be able to cope.

On the other hand, the following sentence, which incorporates the above and is considerably longer, is still acceptable: 'Filling the post presents a problem, because if we appoint from outside we will increase our workforce at a time when we should be cutting back, whereas if we promote John Smith he might not be able to cope with the extra responsibility.' There is still only one idea, but this time it is that filling the post is a problem. The clause about John Smith only qualifies it.

Avoiding awkward sentences

There are several ways in which your sentences can become clumsy and awkward. Sometimes this is because they are incorrect grammatically, but even sentences that are quite correct can occasionally sound wrong. The most common causes of clumsy sentences are:

- incorporating two ideas in one sentence without a conjunction, relative pronoun or semicolon
- putting too many subsidiary clauses before the subject in a periodic sentence
- leaving hanging participles
- letting a sentence get out of parallel

We have already seen the awkward results of **putting more than one idea in a single sentence**, and the more you try to incorporate, the more unwieldy it becomes. Look at the following sentence, for example: 'I am afraid that we are out of stock of that item and are not expecting new stocks for four weeks, at which time we will supply your order unless you decide that you would prefer to cancel, in which case I would be grateful if you would let me know.' This is far too unwieldy, and incorporates four ideas, only two of which are sufficiently related to be included in the same sentence:

- the idea that you are out of stock
- the closely linked idea that you are expecting new stocks in four weeks
- the idea that you will supply the customer's order when the stocks arrive, unless they cancel
- the idea that if they do cancel, you would like them to let you know

So the passage should be written as three sentences: 'I am afraid that we are out of stock of that item and are not expecting new stocks for four weeks. As soon as they arrive, we will supply your order, unless you decide that you would prefer to cancel. If you do decide to cancel, I would be grateful if you would let me know.'

As we have seen, periodic sentences can be useful for building up to a subject and keeping your audience's interest. But **putting too many subsidiary clauses before the subject** can make the sentence unwieldy, as the following sentence shows: 'When I came to the end of my familiarisation exercise, having spent eight week looking in great detail at the way we operate at all levels, during which time I visited all our branches and spoke to most of our staff at all grades, I felt that I knew the company intimately.' There is nothing wrong with this sentence grammatically, but it is awkward to read or to listen to because it takes so long to get to the main clause, 'I felt I knew the company intimately'. Your audience will probably have lost interest by the time you get to the nub of what you want to say.

Hanging participles are participles (in this case the present participle, the '-ing' form of the verb) which start adjectival phrases that have become separated from the nouns they qualify. The following sentence is an example: 'Our February statement has not yet been attended to, showing an outstanding balance of £3,560.' Here, 'showing an outstanding balance of £3,560' is an adjectival phrase which is meant to qualify 'our February statement'. But because the two phrases are separated, it looks awkward – the audience is left wondering what 'showing an outstanding balance of £3,560' refers to. The participle 'showing' is therefore said to be hanging. The sentence should read: 'Our February statement, showing an outstanding balance of £3,560, has not yet been attended to.'

Keeping your sentences **in parallel** means ensuring that you do not combine two different parts of speech in the same construction. It is wrong, for example, to say: 'The meeting was chaotic and a disaster.' 'Chaotic' is an adjective and 'a disaster' is a noun, so the sentence looks clumsy. They must be one or the other. So it should read: 'The meeting was chaotic and disastrous.' Now they are both adjectives, and the sentence is in parallel.

The same rule applies to different forms of the verb. The following is wrong: 'Our aims are to reduce costs and maintaining our service.' 'To reduce' is an infinitive, and 'maintaining' is a present participle. They should both be one or the other. So you can say one of the following:

- Our aims are to reduce costs and to maintain our service.
- Our aims are reducing costs and maintaining our service.

Do not worry about the terms 'infinitive' and 'participle'. Just think of them as the 'to' form and the '-ing' form, and remember that you must use one or the other but not both.

EXERCISE 2

Correct the following sentences.

1. Thanking you for your help in this matter.

2. Please call us for a quote, and we offer a wide range of other services as well.

3. Our latest catalogue is being printed and will be sent to you shortly, including a range of special offers.

4. Having received Mrs Brown's letter, in which she complained about the delay in despatching her order and which you passed on to me, and having conducted a thorough investigation, I am now in a position to report on what went wrong.

5. Enclosed is our quote for the work on your house. Which, as you will see, includes replacing the wooden fascia boards with uPVC.

6. In order to survive we need to:

   a. raise our profile in the market

   b. to increase our productivity

   c. to improve our customer service.

7. I am aware of all the hard work you have put in on behalf of the company, I will consider your request carefully.

8. There appears to have been some misunderstanding regarding my reservation, since I requested a room only, and just for one night, whereas your confirmation is for two nights' bed and breakfast, so I would be grateful if you could amend your records.

Changing the emphasis in a sentence

You can change the emphasis in your sentences simply by changing the order of the words. The parts of a sentence that most people remember are the beginning and the end, so any points you want to emphasise should go there. Consider the following sentence: 'I notified you three weeks ago that I had received the wrong consignment, and despite several telephone calls I have had no response to date.' The emphasis here is on the notification and on the lack of response.

But the writer could have written: 'Three weeks ago, I notified you that I had received the wrong consignment, and I have received no response to date, despite several telephone calls.' Now the emphasis is on the fact that it was three weeks ago that they were notified and on the telephone calls.

Building Sentences into Paragraphs

Just as a sentence should deal with a single idea, or two closely related ideas joined by a conjunction, relative pronoun or semicolon, so a paragraph should deal with just one collection of ideas, one theme or topic. Just as a sentence can become awkward and unwieldy if too many ideas are introduced, so a paragraph will be difficult to follow if there are too many topics competing for the reader's attention; the brain has to store a number of different ideas before it can start working on one of them. When written, it also looks difficult to read, so the reader is almost subconsciously put off before he or she even starts. Look at the passage below.

> Following a study of productivity in the company, we have changed our methods of operation in the Production Department, with the result that productivity has been increased by over 50%. We would now like to introduce similar improvements in other departments. Of course the actual changes will be different from those introduced in the Production Department, because each department has its own operational practices. But the underlying principles should be the same. These principles include streamlining operations, training staff to perform more than one task and empowering employees to find better ways of doing things. As part of this process of empowerment, we would like all staff to consider ways in which they think the work of their departments could be made more efficient. We are aware that when many people hear words like 'efficiency', 'productivity' and 'streamlining' they immediately think of redundancy. We therefore want to reassure all staff from the outset that this exercise is not intended to lead to downsizing and redundancy, voluntary or compulsory. It is simply that if we can increase our productivity we can increase the amount of business we generate from the same number of employees, which has to be good for everyone, not least the employees themselves.

It is not easy to distinguish one thought from another, and reading it is hard work. Now look at how it should have been written.

> Following a study of productivity in the company, we have changed our methods of operation in the Production Department, with the result that productivity has been increased by over 50%. We would now like to introduce similar improvements in other departments.
>
> Of course the actual changes will be different from those introduced in the Production Department, because each department has its own operational practices. But the underlying principles should be the same.
>
> These principles include streamlining operations, training staff to perform more than one task and empowering employees to find better ways of doing things. As part of this process of empowerment, we would like all staff to consider ways in which they think the work of their departments could be made more efficient.
>
> We are aware that when many people hear words like 'efficiency', 'productivity' and 'streamlining' they immediately think of redundancy. We therefore want to reassure all staff from the outset that this exercise is not intended to lead to downsizing and redundancy, voluntary or compulsory. It is simply that if we can increase our productivity we can increase the amount of business we generate from the same number of employees, which has to be good for everyone, not least the employees themselves.

It is very much easier to read, yet all that has happened is that it has been divided into separate paragraphs, each dealing with a particular topic:

- the result of the change in one department and the plan to expand it into others
- the fact that despite different operational practices the underlying principles are the same
- what these principles are, including the desire to empower staff
- the reassurance that the changes will not involve redundancies

Of course, there can be no hard and fast rule about exactly when you should start a new paragraph. People will have different ideas of what constitutes a 'topic'. But it should be fairly clear approximately where one topic ends and the next begins.

Paragraphing

There are a number of reasons why you might use paragraphing, apart from the desire to make your document easier to read.

- to introduce a new topic

- to look at the same topic from a different angle

- to develop one element of a topic

- for special emphasis

- to move your argument forward

EXERCISE 12

Rewrite the following letter, using the same words and sentences, but dividing it into paragraphs.

Dear Mr Iqbal

Following our conversation last week, I would like to confirm the arrangements for your sales conference on 15 and 16 May. We have reserved the small conference room for you. This seats 40 people, and since there will only be 30 attending there will be plenty of room for everyone. We will provide seating and tables in a horseshoe layout, as you requested. We will also provide a flip chart and easel and an overhead projector. If you also need a digital projector, one can be made available; you need only ask me on the day. We will serve coffee and tea at 11 a.m. and 3.30 p.m. and lunch at 1 p.m. on both days, in a separate room. Lunch menus are attached. I understand that only the wine with the meal is to be charged to your company, and that any other drinks should be paid for. A private bar will be set aside for your use. I have also reserved 15 rooms with private baths for those who are staying overnight. I look forward to seeing you on the 15th, and thank you for choosing our hotel for your venue.

Yours sincerely

Keith Blackstone
Conference Manage

You can also use paragraphing to indicate that you are about to look at the same topic but from a different point of view, as the following extract shows:

I can offer you a complete service – not just office cleaning but also laundry and towel replacement. I will even look after your reception area for you, ensuring that your plants are cared for and that there is an attractive collection of magazines available.

Of course, if all you want is an office cleaning service, I can provide that on its own, and I think you will find my rates and my service the best in town.

The first paragraph deals with the services this person offers. The second also deals with those services, so it is in fact covering the same topic. But it covers it from a different perspective – that of a customer who does not want a complete service.

Paragraphing can also help you develop a topic, or an element or concept within it. For example:

For all these reasons, our strategy must be one of expansion. We do not yet fully exploit our potential in the market, and there are many areas where there is room to improve our performance. The most important, and potentially the most profitable, of these is the export market.

Exports account for only 15 per cent of total sales. With careful planning, the right personnel and a certain amount of investment, we could increase that to 25 per cent within a year.

Here the writer is continuing with the same topic, but is developing an element of it (exports) until it becomes a topic in its own right.

Many people, when planning their documents, actually list the topics so that they know what is to go into each paragraph. This can be a very useful technique, especially if you are using the list method of outline. You can then develop a paragraph out of each point on your list.

Paragraph length

As I have indicated, there are no precise rules about what constitutes a 'topic', so a certain amount of flexibility is possible in the length of your paragraphs. Short paragraphs are generally preferable to long ones. As you can see in the above examples, shorter paragraphs *look* easier to read, and if your readers *think* a document is going to be easy to read, then the battle for their attention is half won. If, on the other hand, you have very long paragraphs, your document will look boring, and you will have an uphill battle convincing your readers that it is not.

Very short, single-sentence paragraphs can be used for emphasis. They tend to bring your readers up short, to make them sit up and take notice. Look at the following passage:

I spoke to you on the telephone on 16 January. You said that there had been problems with your bank, and promised that payment would be made by 20 January.

It was not.

I telephoned you again on 25 January, but you were not available. Your assistant told me that there was a cheque in the post, and that it would be with me by the following day.

It was not.

You can see how the single-sentence paragraphs emphasise the fact that payment has not been received. The repetition is particularly effective in hammering home the message. But use this device sparingly. Its effectiveness lies in the fact that it is unusual. If you use it too much it loses its 'shock' value, and your documents will just look disjointed.

As with sentences, variety is the key, so it is usually best to vary the length of your paragraphs. A document consisting solely of short paragraphs will be almost as hard to read as one with only long paragraphs. Much will depend, of course, on the topics you are discussing, but if you find that you have a number of very short paragraphs, it might be a good idea to check to see whether they really do each cover a complete topic.

A lot will also depend on the document. Paragraphs in a report will usually be longer than those in a letter or memo, because the report itself will usually be longer, and the subject will usually be discussed at greater length.

The topic sentence

Each paragraph should have what is called a topic sentence, one that encapsulates what the paragraph is going to be about. It should be at the beginning of the paragraph, usually the first sentence. Look at some of the examples above, and you will see the topic sentences:

- 'I can offer you a complete service ...' tells you that the paragraph is going to be about the service.
- 'Exports account for only 15% of total sales' tells you that the paragraph is going to be about exports.
- 'I spoke to you on the telephone ...' tells you that the paragraph is going to be about the telephone conversation.

The advantage of topic sentences is that they make it easier to follow the flow of your document by telling the reader what to expect from each paragraph. They might even be based on the points in your list outline.

Expanding your theme

As we have seen, the topic sentence introduces the theme, but you need to expand from that into a full paragraph. There are several techniques for this, depending on what you want to say. These are the most common:

- **Arguing your case**. You might make a statement in your topic sentence and then explain it in the rest of the paragraph. For example: 'We must be totally confident that you will be able to meet our deadline. It is extremely costly to have our machines lying idle. It is not only a question of having to pay operators when there is no work to be done, but the shut-down and start-up costs are extremely high.' The topic sentence makes the statement, and the rest of the paragraph sets out the reasons why the deadline must be met.
- **Presenting the background**. Your topic sentence might outline the subject of the paragraph, with the rest of the paragraph providing additional information: 'Nigeria is

one of our most important sales areas. With a population estimated at 150 million, it represents a huge market, and one which we have not yet fully tapped. It is a country of entrepreneurs, with a thirst for consumer goods. Although it has been through several phases of upheaval, it is at present reasonably stable.' The topic sentence signals that the paragraph is going to be about Nigeria as a sales area, and the rest of the paragraph gives further information about the country.

- **Reinforcing your message**. You might use the rest of the paragraph to emphasise the point made in your topic sentence by repeating it from a different perspective: 'Our costs are rising at a worrying rate. Raw material prices increased by 15% this year. Overheads increased by 20%, partly because of an increase in our rent. And payroll costs increased by 10%, even though we actually saw a fall in the number of staff.' Here the second, third and fourth sentences give examples of the way costs have risen, thus reinforcing the message of the topic sentence.

- **Outlining the consequences**. You might make a statement in your topic sentence and then use the rest of the paragraph to show what the results might be: 'We have not met our turnover budget this year. This means that we will have to reduce our overheads substantially next year. Redundancies will be inevitable.'

- **Giving your reasons**. You might outline a situation in the topic sentence, and then use the rest of the paragraph to give your reasons: 'I am afraid that we are not able to supply your order at present. There has been an industrial dispute at the factory which manufactures these items. We are trying to locate another source of supply, but have been unable to do so yet.'

These are only the most common techniques for expanding your paragraph, and they are given here as suggestions only. Do not feel that that you *must* use them. There may be situations which you feel do not fit any of these techniques. In that case, develop your paragraph in the way you think suits the situation best. As long as the information is presented in a logical way, it does not matter a great deal what technique you use.

Paragraph Headings

Whether you use headings for your paragraphs is largely a matter of personal preference, but when deciding whether to use them or not, bear the following in mind:

- Headings usually interrupt the flow of the text, so they should only be used when they serve a genuine purpose.

- They can often be useful to the reader 'skimming' the document, as they will give a quick idea of the contents.

- They are usually inappropriate for short documents, like most letters, memos and e-mails, when the reader can get a good idea of the contents by reading the whole thing. In these cases they simply interfere with the flow.

- The can make a complex document easier to read by highlighting the main points.

- They make cross-referencing easier.

Getting the flow right

We have seen how you can expand your paragraph by developing the subject of your topic sentence logically. The same goes for the development of your document as a whole. It should flow logically, one topic leading on to the next. Conduct your audience through it without jumping from subject to subject. Each paragraph should have a natural connection with the previous one.

There are two ways of making this connection:

- by taking an idea from the last sentence of one paragraph and using it to start the next
- by using various forms of words to signal the direction your argument or narrative is going to take

Let us look at each of these in more detail. Repeating an idea from one paragraph at the start of the next creates a very smooth flow. There is a clear link. Look at this passage:

At Sunnyside Garden Centre we pride ourselves on being able to satisfy even the most demanding of customers. That is why we carry the widest range of tools in the area.

We have something for every job, from powerful motor mowers to simple trowels.

Can you see how the idea of the wide range of tools is repeated in the first sentence of the second paragraph, thus creating a smooth transition from one paragraph to the next?

You can make the repetition even more direct by repeating one of the words in the previous sentence, or by replacing it with a pronoun or a synonym (a word with a similar meaning). So the second paragraph could have begun with:

- We have tools for every job ...
- We have them for every job ...
- We have equipment for every job ...

Very often, however, the new paragraph cannot be introduced by simply repeating an idea from the previous one. You may be about to change direction, or look at the same topic from a different angle. But you still need to make a link with what has gone before. You can use different expressions to make that link and indicate where you are going. Which one you use depends on what purpose the new paragraph serves, but here are a few examples.

- **Expanding on what has gone before**. The following expressions will indicate that you are going to explain your previous paragraph more fully.
    - The reason is ...
    - You will understand that ...
    - This means that ...
    - For example ...
    - Indeed ...
    - What is more ...

- **Changing direction**. The following will indicate that you are going to look at the subject from a different angle.

  - However ...
  - Even so ...
  - Nevertheless ...
  - On the other hand ...

- **Moving forward**. The following will tell your audience that you are going on to the next stage of the discussion.

  - Therefore ...
  - Similarly ...
  - As a result ...

- **Ending your document**. The following indicate that this is the last paragraph, and that you are bringing your document to a neat close.

  - Finally ...
  - To summarise ....

Below is a letter without any linking devices. Can you see how disjointed it looks?

SUNNYSIDE GARDEN CENTRE
Oak Tree Cross, Towerbridge Road, King's Beech, KB5 6CD
Tel. 01678 901234

27 March 20XX

Dear Customer

Spring is on its way, and with it the chance to get out and enjoy your garden. Whether you have a large allotment or just a patio, now is the time to start sowing and planting so as to get the most out of it later in the year.

Your garden will certainly need digging, composting and fertilising in preparation for the growing season.

Why not come down to Sunnyside Garden Centre? We have plants and seeds galore, from fruit trees to phlox seeds and from artichokes to amaryllis, together with every conceivable medium to grow them in. And if you aren't sure of the best varieties for your needs, you only have to ask. Many of our staff are experts in various fields.

We can give you a complete service, whatever your needs. We have sprays to control pests and diseases you didn't even know existed, a complete range of organic products and the widest selection of tools in the area.

Any new product we stock is tested by our staff before we sell it, so that we can personally recommend everything on our shelves.

We pride ourselves on being able to satisfy even the most demanding of customers. Our motto is 'Try harder' and we do. Our staff are friendly and helpful, but never pushy.

We haven't forgotten the children. We have just opened a new section devoted entirely to swings, slides, climbing frames and other equipment to make your garden fun to be in, whatever your age.

Do pay us a visit. We look forward to seeing you soon.

Yours sincerely

Jack Kemp
Managing Director

Now look at the same letter, but with linking devices added, and see how much more smoothly it flows.

SUNNYSIDE GARDEN CENTRE
Oak Tree Cross, Towerbridge Road, King's Beech, KB5 6CD
Tel. 01678 901234

27 March 20XX

Dear Customer

Spring is on its way, and with it the chance to get out and enjoy your garden. Whether you have a large allotment or just a patio, now is the time to start sowing and planting so as to get the most out of it later in the year.

It is not only sowing and planting you should be thinking of. Your garden will certainly need digging, composting and fertilising in preparation for the growing season.

So why not come down to Sunnyside Garden Centre? We have plants and seeds galore, from fruit trees to phlox seeds and from artichokes to amaryllis, together with every conceivable medium to grow them in. And if you aren't sure of the best varieties for your needs, you only have to ask. Many of our staff are experts in various fields.

What this means is that we can give you a complete service, whatever your needs. We have sprays to control pests and diseases you didn't even know existed, a complete range of organic products and the widest selection of tools in the area.

We have equipment for every job, from motor mowers to simple trowels. Any new product we stock is tested by our staff before we sell it, so that we can personally recommend everything on our shelves.

What is more, we pride ourselves on being able to satisfy even the most demanding of customers. Our motto is 'Try harder' and we do. Our staff are friendly and helpful, but never pushy.

Finally, we haven't forgotten the children. We have just opened a new section devoted entirely to swings, slides, climbing frames and other equipment to make your garden fun to be in, whatever your age.

So do pay us a visit. We look forward to seeing you soon.

Yours sincerely

Jack Kemp
Managing Director

The devices used are:

- 'It is not only sowing and planting ...' – repetition, combined with the expression 'not only' to indicate that the writer is going to expand on this subject.
- 'So why not come down ...?' – to indicate that he is going on to the next stage.

- 'What this means is ...' – to indicate that he is going to explain further.
- 'We have equipment ...' – repetition of the idea from the last sentence of the previous paragraph.
- 'Finally, we haven't forgotten ...' – to indicate that he is reaching his conclusion.

How Sentences and Paragraphs Affect the Way You Speak

The preparation necessary for a conversation, verbal report or presentation will be different from that for a written document, for three reasons:

- Spoken business English does not have to be quite as formal and grammatical.
- You are unlikely to plan *exactly* what you are going to say, down to the last word, so at least some of your sentence composition will be done as you speak.
- It is easier to get away with the occasional 'non-sentence' in spoken English.

Nevertheless, even in spoken English, it is necessary to take *some* care over your sentence and paragraph construction if you want to make yourself quite clear to your audience.

Sentences

It is easier to get away with using awkward or incorrect sentences in spoken English than poor paragraph construction. Let us look, for example, at one of the examples of a non-sentence above: 'There is only one problem. The cost.' As we saw, 'the cost' is not a sentence, because it does not have a predicate. The correct construction should have been, 'There is only one problem: the cost.' However, when speaking, the difference between the length of pause required after a colon and that required after a full stop is so small that when speaking it will not be noticed (for more on the pauses indicated by punctuation marks, see Chapter 8).

However, some awkward sentences could cause problems, even when spoken. Let us look at another example quoted in the section on sentences above: 'I enclose your latest statement, I would like to point out that there is an amount of £135 outstanding.' As we saw, this is wrong because there are two ideas, but they are only separated by a comma. And this could sound wrong, even when spoken, because a comma calls for a shorter pause than a semicolon or some kind of connecting word, so your sentence could sound as though the ideas are running into each other, making it difficult for the audience to differentiate them. And since you should be aiming to make your audience's job easier, it is best to avoid this kind of problem by sticking to the rules governing sentences with more than one idea.

Having too many subsidiary clauses or phrases before the subject is actually likely to confuse listeners even more than readers. Here again is the example of this problem we looked at earlier: 'When I came to the end of my familiarisation exercise, having spent eight weeks looking in great detail at the way we operate at all levels, during which time I visited all our branches and spoke to most of our staff at all grades, I felt that I knew the company intimately.' At least if such a sentence is written down, the readers can, with some difficulty, work out what is meant. However, when spoken, the listeners do not have the luxury of being able to go over it again – if they are confused the first time, they will remain confused. It is also possible for the speaker to become so bogged down in subsidiary clauses that they themselves become confused as to what the main point is!

Because of the relative informality of spoken English, hanging participles and sentences that are out of parallel do not sound as awkward when spoken as they look when written. So although you should always aim to speak grammatically, sentences such as 'Our aims are to reduce costs and maintaining customer satisfaction' are likely to cause less offence when spoken than when written.

Paragraphs

It is more important to ensure that you do not ignore paragraphing when preparing to speak. You should divide your material into paragraphs in exactly the same way as you would if you were preparing a written document, even though you may not prepare the exact sentences you intend to use in each paragraph.

The first reason for this is that paragraphing allows you and your audience to pause and collect your thoughts or absorb what has just been said before you move on to the next topic. That is what a paragraph break is for, and just as readers pause at the end of a paragraph, so should you when speaking. We have all come across people who speak in a constant stream, without a pause and with one subject merging apparently seamlessly into the next. It is not only very difficult to follow, it can also be very tiring! Moreover, it makes two-way communication very difficult, as the other person has no opportunity to ask questions or raise points of clarification. Try speaking the following passage (or even better, ask someone else to read it to you), and you will see the problem.

What I am proposing is that we take a completely new look at the way we run our organisation. At the moment, we run it on rather paternalistic lines, which may have been fine when the company was first set up, but times and attitudes have changed since then. We are also no longer a small family firm; perhaps paternalism is more acceptable in such circumstances. What we need is a complete change of culture, with more decisions being made at lower levels in the hierarchy and with the employees being empowered to take action on their own initiative. Such a major change might meet with some resistance among certain senior managers, who might resent what they see as a loss of power – and possibly even among some lower down the scale, who are not used to being asked to make decisions, and could feel somewhat vulnerable. It therefore needs to be handled carefully and sensitively. Nevertheless, I am convinced that it must be done, even if in the process we lose some of our longer-serving employees, who cannot accept the change. If it is not, we will almost certainly be unable to recruit staff of the calibre we need if we are to move forward – staff who are innovative, and who are not afraid to take risks.

Not only is it difficult to follow the train of thought because the subjects merge into each other, but if the listener wanted clarification of any of the points raised, they would not know when (or how) to break into the flow.

When speaking, you also still need a topic sentence – indeed it could be argued that it is even more important when speaking than when writing. At least the reader of a document will eventually be able to work out what the paragraph is about without a topic sentence, but someone listening to you speaking will need this indicator at the start.

The same applies to signalling devices; if you do not signal your intentions at the start of a paragraph in a document it will look disjointed, but at least the reader will be able to work out where you are taking the subject with a bit of effort. However, if you omit the signalling devices when you are speaking, you are likely to lose your listeners. They will not understand whether you are expanding on the topic of the last paragraph, changing direction or moving your argument forward.

What this means is that, although the relative informality of spoken English enables you to get away with less grammatical sentences than in a written document, you should try to speak as grammatically as possible without sounding artificial. And you should certainly not ignore the rules regarding paragraphing – they are, if anything, more important in spoken work.

CHAPTER 5
Good business style

So far, we have discussed the 'mechanics' of business communication – planning, layout and construction. We now come to the content – what you want to say and how you are going to say it, in other words your style. There are two elements to style:

- your tone
- your words

Both of these are important in giving your communication the right quality, and in achieving the reaction you want.

Using the Right Tone

Although your tone will to a certain extent depend on the words you use, it is also influenced by the way you use them. If you set out to be friendly, for example, you will express yourself in a way that conveys that impression, whether you are speaking or writing. If you are not pleased about something, you will choose forms of expression that make that clear.

Be sincere

One of the most important things about getting your tone right is sincerity. Whether you are trying to make a sale, replying to an enquiry or making a complaint, you must believe in what you are saying, and that belief must be made clear. Look at the following passage: 'We acknowledge with thanks receipt of your recent communication, and enclose a copy of our catalogue as requested. Should you have any queries, the undersigned will be pleased to assist you.' Reading this, do you get the feeling that the 'undersigned' really *will* be pleased to assist you? It does not sound much like it. The language is so stilted and formal that it becomes merely a form of words, without real meaning. This may have been acceptable in the past, but in today's more informal business climate, it would be considered almost rude.

Now look at this: 'I would like to thank you most sincerely for taking the time to write to us, and for giving us the opportunity to serve you. Here is your very own copy of our catalogue, to browse through at your leisure. If you have any queries, I would love to help you. I'll be waiting for your call.' This writer goes too far in the other direction. The tone is too gushing, too good to be true. First, if you are being sincere, the last thing you should do is *say* so. If you have to tell people that you are being sincere, then you have failed to get your sincerity across. Second, do you really believe that someone is sitting in their office, just waiting for your call? And is there anything special about having your 'very own copy' of a catalogue rather than just a 'copy'?

Now see how you can say the same thing simply, straightforwardly, and yet with sincerity: 'Thank you for your letter. I am pleased to enclose our latest catalogue, for you to browse through at your leisure. If you have any queries I would be happy to help, so just give me a call.' This is not over-formal, but nor does it gush. It does not give the impression that the writer is merely using a form of words, but it also does not sound as though he or she is trying too hard. In other words it sounds sincere.

Be clear

Your communication should be as clear, as precise and as direct as possible. The tone, the way you use your words and sentences, can usually help to achieve this.

Testing for Clarity

To see whether what you are going to say is as clear as it should be, ask these questions.

- If a particular point is unusual or especially important, how are you planning to emphasise it?

- Are there any vague expressions?

- Are there any euphemisms?

- Are any words or sentences ambiguous?

- Have you got all the information required?

A common mistake is to try to emphasise important points with lengthy explanations. This is more likely to turn people off what you are saying. It is much better to use short, punchy, one-sentence paragraphs or repeat the word or idea once or twice in short sentences. In certain circumstances, you might use underlining or block capitals, but these devices should be used sparingly, otherwise they lose their effect.

Clarity and precision also mean avoiding vague terms and euphemisms. We saw in Chapter 1 how Jane Lee, in her verbal report to her colleagues, referred to a 'good' meeting with Carlos Rodriguez. You would probably be able to get away with this in spoken communication, because your audience could ask for clarification. But it would nevertheless be better to be more precise, and in a written document it would be essential. You should say what made the meeting good: was it productive, did it clarify the issues, did it lead to an agreement, or did you just get on well with the other people there?

Euphemisms are a form of vagueness: at best they use more words than a direct statement and at worst, because of their lack of directness, they can be misunderstood. They also give the impression that you are trying to hide something. So do not say, 'Profits showed a negative trend' when you mean 'We made a loss', or even when you mean 'Profits were down on last year.' Not only does it sound as though you are trying to hide your poor performance behind the euphemism, but as we have seen, it could mean either of two things.

It is not only euphemisms that can sometimes be ambiguous. Even apparently straightforward words and sentences might be capable of being understood in more than one way. So if, for example, you use the word 'sales', is it clear from your context whether you mean sales value or sales volume; and can people tell whether 'improvement in profitability' means increased profits or higher profit margins? You should also not say something like 'I need to know what our costs will be by the end of this month' if you mean 'I need to know by the end of this month what our costs will be.' In the first sentence, 'by the end of this month' refers to the costs, not to when you need to know.

Finally, clarity requires that you give all the information that is necessary so that there is no scope for misunderstanding or confusion. In a quotation, for example, you need to ensure that you describe the goods or services for which you are quoting precisely, and give the prices, the cost of any extras, delivery time, etc.

Be brief

As we saw in Chapter 1, one of the cardinal rules in business communication is brevity. Business people do not want to waste time reading or listening to a lot of superfluous verbiage. They want information, but they want to be able to absorb it as quickly as possible.

One way of achieving brevity, of course, is to use as few words as possible. You should not, however, let brevity get in the way of clarity; if shortening your communication makes it incomplete or difficult to follow, then it is not worth doing. Nor should you choose brevity before politeness; if using fewer words means omitting some of the courtesies, then again it is not worth it.

There are three main causes of wordiness in business communications:

- circumlocution
- vague qualifiers
- padding

Let us look at each in turn. Circumlocution means using a long expression when a short one will do. For example, someone trying to sound important might say, 'I have caused enquiries to be made with a view to establishing the reasons for our inability to supply your order.' This could be said quite simply in half the words: 'I have enquired into the reasons why we were unable to supply your order.' The first version does not sound important, nor does it add weight to what the person is saying. It simply sounds pompous and long-winded.

Vague qualifiers are adjectives and adverbs that do not mean anything. These include 'really', 'good', 'nice' and similar words which are usually used because the writer or speaker cannot be bothered to think of anything more precise or simply because they are handy fillers. Using such words as fillers in conjunction with more precise terms in speech will usually be acceptable, because spoken English tends to be more informal and they can give you time to gather your thoughts. However, even in speech they should not be used *instead* of precise terms. And they should not be used, even as fillers, in written documents.

An example of using these words as fillers is in the description of a meeting as being 'really productive'. Is this any different from a 'productive' meeting? Is it as productive as a 'very productive' meeting? It has no meaning, so it should not be used in a written document – although it might be acceptable when speaking, as 'productive' is precise enough to convey the specific idea. But what do you make of the expression 'a good candidate'? Whether you are speaking or writing, this is not precise or clear enough to be of any value. Does it describe someone who interviews well, someone who is suitable for the job, someone with the right qualifications, or all three?

The use of vague qualifiers as fillers is one example of padding – using words and expressions that serve no useful purpose. Longer expressions that fall into this category include 'It should be noted that ...' and 'I must say that ...' Again, you can get away with using such expressions when speaking, as long as you do not do so too often, but they should not be used in written communications.

You also need to be careful; although most expressions like this are unnecessary, some can serve a useful purpose. For example, 'You will appreciate that ...' sounds like padding, but it can be used to get the reader on your side. For example, if you want to explain why you are unable to give a customer a higher discount, you can say: 'You will appreciate that our discounts are already generous. Our margins are therefore already tight, and any increase in discount would erode them yet further.' This appeals to your customer as a reasonable and intelligent person who will understand these problems. So although 'You will appreciate' is really padding, it does serve a purpose.

Achieving a conversational tone

There was a time when all business correspondence was expected to be formal and impersonal, but that is no longer the case – indeed this kind of style is now regarded as positively discourteous. The preferred style now is more informal and conversational; people write almost as they would speak – perhaps not quite as informally and certainly not using slang, but nevertheless in a friendlier manner. So think how you would react if you received different styles of communication, and write or speak accordingly.

Techniques for Achieving a Conversational Tone in Letters

- If possible, address your correspondent by name.

- Make the letter personal – from *you*, rather than the company – so use 'I' rather than 'we'.

- Avoid formal expressions such as 'We acknowledge receipt'.

- Use the active rather than the passive voice: 'I have made enquiries', rather than 'Enquiries have been made.' The former sounds friendlier, the latter less personal.

- If you are in the wrong, admit it and apologise.

- If your correspondent is in the wrong, say so tactfully and politely.

EXERCISE 14

Below is a letter answering a customer's complaint. What do you think is wrong with its tone? Write the kind of letter you think should have been sent.

CARSTAIRS CLOTHING COMPANY
43 Gorton Road, Marsby, MB2 4HY
Tel. 01921 143267

26 August 20XX

Mrs A. Maxwell
13 Thrixton Crescent
Charterborough
LT14 6TU

Dear Madam

We are in receipt of your letter of 15 August regarding the return of a dress, item 456732. On investigation, it appears that the dress was indeed received. Your account has therefore been credited with the appropriate amount.

We are only able to entertain claims for compensation if actual financial loss has been incurred.
This is quite obviously not the case in this instance.

Yours faithfully

Catherine Porter
Customer Relations Manager

The right tone for your purpose

We need to use different tones for different kinds of communication. We usually do this naturally when we speak – if we have made an error we automatically adopt an apologetic tone, when we are complaining we are forceful, when we are making a request, we are conciliatory. In writing, however, it sometimes requires a bit more thought to get the tone right for the occasion. The key is to think of the reaction you want – what you want to achieve – and adopt the most appropriate tone. So a sales letter should be enthusiastic, a letter demanding payment firm, a report persuasive.

Not only will your tone change according to the nature of your document, it will also be different for different readers. For example, a request to your Managing Director might be expressed as follows: 'I wonder whether you would agree to the company paying something towards the staff's Christmas party this year.'

On the other hand, a request to a subordinate might be expressed differently: 'Please could you let me have the costings for the product launch by next Tuesday?'

No matter what you are writing, however, and no matter to whom it is addressed, you should always be polite. You can make your point clearly, but never be rude. You are more likely to get the response you want if you are polite than if you are offensive. Even when complaining, you can be forceful yet polite, for example: 'This is the third time I have had to write to you about this matter. I am afraid that if I do not receive a satisfactory reply within the next week I shall be forced to take the necessary legal action.' And if you are a manager it is not only unproductive but also extremely unfair to be rude to your subordinates, as they cannot answer you in kind.

Rudeness often goes hand in hand with emotion, and you should never be emotional in business communication. Argue your case forcefully, show your displeasure, but do not let emotion dictate your tone. This is particularly important when speaking – it is all too easy to get carried away and say things without thinking. But if you allow emotion to dictate what you say you are unlikely to get the reaction you want.

Emphasise the positive

It is a good idea, when you sit down to plan your communication, to think of both the positive and the negative sides of what you want to say, and to emphasise the positive. This does not mean that you should ignore the negative, especially if you are writing a report or making a presentation. But by emphasising the positive and perhaps trying to ameliorate any negative aspects your communication will come over as positive, which will help to get the reaction you want.

This applies even to something like a letter making a final demand for payment. Look at the letter below.

ABC OFFICE EQUIPMENT
54 Union Street, Kingston St Mary, GM14 6FD
Tel. 01321 908765

16 November 20XX

Mr Harold Mills
Financial Director
NWS Manufacturing
NWS House
Kingston St Mary
GM14 7TP

Dear Mr Mills

I am very sorry to see that, despite my letters of 31 August, 15 September and 30 September, as well as a number of telephone calls, we have still not been paid the amount outstanding on your account. Perhaps I could remind you that the sum involved is £1,201.50, and that it has been outstanding since June.

Our normal policy when payment has been overdue for so long without any reason being offered is to pursue our claim through the courts. I am sure that you would not want the embarrassment and publicity that this would entail, and for our part we would be sorry to have to take that kind of action against a company which has been a valued customer for a long time. We are therefore prepared to delay any action for one week more. If we receive payment within that time, then we can both be spared the unpleasantness of legal action.

I look forward to receiving your cheque.

Yours sincerely

Lionel Grantham
Credit Controller

This is as firm as it needs to be, and Lionel Grantham sets out quite clearly the consequences of non-payment. But while doing so, he emphasises the positive side of paying (Harold Mills will avoid the embarrassment of being taken to court). And he says, 'If we receive payment within that time, then we can both be spared the unpleasantness of legal action', rather than the more negative 'If we do not receive payment within that time, then we will be forced to take legal action.' The result is a positive, polite, yet forceful letter, which is far more likely to achieve the result Lionel wants than a rude, negative one.

This idea of emphasising the positive side of what you have to say applies to all communications. For example, if you are telling your clients about a reorganisation of your company, do not just say, 'I am writing to tell you about some changes we have made.' It is better to say, 'We have made some changes in our organisation that will, I am sure, improve our service to you.' This introduces a positive element, which makes a favourable impression on your audience.

Choosing the Right Words

When choosing your words, bear in mind the rules of business English: brevity, clarity and directness. Use words that help achieve these aims. The secret is to keep it simple. For example, you should say 'buy' rather than 'purchase', and 'try' rather than 'endeavour'. And *never* use a word unless you are sure you know exactly what it means – you could be saying something very different from what you intended! The main reason why people use long, complex or unusual words is that they think they are impressive. Do not be tempted, because they are not impressive, just long-winded or pompous.

Of course, in achieving a conversational style, you should not slip over into slang, even when speaking. If you do, you will give the impression either that you do not know the difference between slang and good English, or that you do not care. So avoid expressions like 'OK', 'fed up with' or 'on the dot'.

There are four common faults that will make your communication seem either long-winded or sloppy:

- jargon
- tautology
- unnecessary abstract nouns
- clichés

Jargon

Jargon is technical language that is specific to a group or profession. Sometimes it is necessary, especially in the scientific and technical fields. Even in business writing, there may be times when you need to use a technical term that is clearly understood. But most business jargon simply complicates your communication. You must differentiate between acceptable business vocabulary (such as 'contingency planning' or 'bill of exchange') and 'management-speak' (such terms as 'interface' and 'downturn'). You should also avoid 'commercialese' (expressions like 'we are in receipt of' and 'aforementioned'). Do not even use acceptable jargon with lay people unless you are certain they will understand what you mean.

Jargon is very difficult to eradicate; new words and expressions are being added to the business person's vocabulary all the time, and many of them are unnecessary jargon. You need to be on your guard against them because initially they can sound quite impressive – until you realise that they do not actually add anything, or that they are unclear or imprecise. So avoid any expressions which do not have a precise meaning that could not be more simply expressed in plain English. Here are some examples of both jargon and 'commercialese':

- at this moment in time
- assuring you of our best attention
- advise us (instead of 'tell us')
- as per your order
- commence (instead of 'begin')
- forward (instead of 'send')
- flag up
- touch base
- in the loop
- thinking outside the box
- get your ducks in a row

Of course, English is an ever-changing language, and today's jargon may become tomorrow's acceptable English. In the past, when the suffix -ise was put at the end of an adjective or noun to turn it into a verb, the resulting word was regarded as jargon. But today words like 'globalise' and 'computerise' have entered everyday language. There can therefore be no hard and fast rules, but perhaps the best guide is the one I gave at the beginning of this section: if a word or expression does not have a specific meaning that cannot be expressed in plain English, do not use it.

Tautology

Tautology means unnecessary repetition – saying the same thing in different words. Some people use it to emphasise a point, but there are better ways of emphasising something. Tautology is poor style; it serves no useful purpose, and simply makes you sound long-winded. Here are some examples of tautological expressions commonly used in business communication:

- the true facts (if facts were not true, they would not be facts)
- grateful thanks (thanks are an expression of gratitude)
- my personal opinion (how could your opinion be anything but personal?)
- close proximity (proximity is closeness)

There are two other common errors, which are not strictly tautology, but which nevertheless add unnecessary words. The first is the expression 'and/or'. This is usually used when the writer means 'and'; it is sometimes used to mean 'or', but there are very few occasions when you actually mean 'and' *and* 'or' at the same time. It is therefore ambiguous as well as long-winded.

The second error is putting 'as' before certain words, as in 'as from', 'as and when', and 'as yet'. These expressions mean exactly the same without the 'as'. 'As from' means 'from', 'as and when' means 'when', and 'as yet' means 'yet'. 'As yet' does sometimes serve a purpose. It can be used at the beginning of a sentence to make the meaning clear. For example, in the sentence 'Yet you have failed to supply our order', 'yet' means 'despite everything'. If you want to say 'until now', then you *must* use 'as yet': 'As yet you have failed to supply our order.' But this is the only time that 'as yet' should be used.

Unnecessary abstract nouns

There will obviously be times when you will need to use abstract nouns, but many people seem to be unable to resist using them at every opportunity. However, one of the rules of business communication is to be direct, and the concrete is usually more direct than the abstract.

Most abstract nouns sound vague and often pompous. They also usually have the effect of making your communication long-winded. Particularly bad are nouns derived from verbs. There are examples of these in the following:

- The reconciliation of your account is in progress. (Your account is being reconciled.)
- The achievement of our sales target will not be possible without greater effort on your part. (We need greater effort on your part to achieve our sales target.)
- A quick settlement of your account would be appreciated. (Please settle your account quickly.)

Clichés

Clichés are expressions that have been used so often that they have become old and overworked. They will make your communication seem artificial and insincere, giving the impression that you could not be bothered to think of an original expression. Here are some examples:

- Be that as it may ...
- Needless to say ...
- I have explored every avenue.
- The fact of the matter is ...
- Far be it from me ...
- Last but not least ...

Using Abbreviations in Written Communication

Abbreviations should generally be avoided, as they may not always be understood. They can also give the impression that you cannot be bothered to write the words out in full. There are, however, some exceptions, such as following:

- some standard abbreviations that have almost become words in their own right, like Mr, Mrs, Dr (as a title, not as a description of someone's profession), No., plc, Ltd

- countries and organisation that are usually referred to by their initials – the USA, the UK, the EU, the CBI, the TUC, the BBC

- Co., when it is part of a company's name, as in John Smith & Co. (but in all other cases, write out 'company')

- the ampersand (&), also when it is part of an organisation's name, as in Jones & Brown plc (but in all other cases use 'and')

You should avoid using 'etc'. Your communication should be specific, and 'etc.' gives the impression that you do not know all the facts or are too lazy to give them. If the list of things you want to mention is too long, use 'for example' or 'such as', rather than 'etc.' So instead of 'We need to discuss discount, payment terms, minimum order quantities, etc.' you should say, 'We need to discuss issues such as discount, payment terms and minimum, order quantities.'

Speaking Clearly

Do not think that style is something you need to be concerned about only when writing. You may be a little more informal when speaking than when writing, but your style is nevertheless important if you are going to get your message across clearly.

EXERCISE 15

Identify the stylistic errors in the following letter.

BURGESS FINANCIAL SERVICES
4 Market House, Union Street Warchester, WR1 4ST
Tel. 01234 567890

24 October 20XX

Mr Stephen Morris
24 College Road
Warchester
WR2 3UV

Dear Mr Morris

This is to confirm my telephone conversation with you this morning regarding your request for a quote for car insurance.

I have taken on board your requirements and conducted a thorough investigation of all the options open to you, leaving no stone unturned and looking at all the policies on offer. Attached are the details of the best policy I have been able to find for your needs. As I said on the phone, it provides all the standard cover you asked for. The downside is that in the event that you needed to utilise your vehicle for business travel you would need to take out a completely new policy.

If you are happy with the terms as outlined, I would be grateful if you could let me have your cheque for the first premium at your earliest convenience, so that provision can be made for cover as from the beginning of next month.

Yours sincerely

Martin Burgess

Tone

Your tone is particularly important when speaking, as your audience can *hear* your tone. For example, although you might be able to fake sincerity, firmness or enthusiasm when writing, it is very difficult to do so when speaking, so you must ensure that you really believe in what you are saying. Circumlocutions, too, give an even worse impression when spoken than when written – they sound pretentious. You should also avoid euphemisms; at best they also sound pretentious, and at worst they sound as though you are trying to mislead your audience.

You might get away with vague qualifiers like 'good' or 'nice' because your audience can ask you to clarify your point, but they nevertheless give the impression that you are not clear in your own mind about exactly what you mean. You might be able to use the occasional word or sentence that can be misunderstood for the same reason. But if you do this too often your communication will become disjointed as you constantly have to stop to clarify what you mean, and you will appear vague and ill-prepared.

The only aspect of achieving the right tone that is really acceptable in spoken English, therefore, is the use of padding. This enables you to gather your thoughts, and gives your audience an opportunity to absorb what you have said so far. However, it should not be carried too far, as it could make your communication unnecessarily long.

Words

As with your tone, you need to pay almost as much attention to the words you use when speaking as you do when writing. Of course, you can be more conversational and informal, as we have seen, but not at the expense of clarity, brevity and directness. So although you might introduce the occasional colloquialism, you should still avoid jargon; like some of the aspects of tone we discussed above, it can sound pretentious without adding anything to what you are saying. Abstract nouns should be avoided where possible for the same reason – 'The processing of your order is being attended to with all due speed' sounds awfully pretentious when what you actually mean is 'We are processing your order as quickly as possible.'

Tautology might be acceptable in certain circumstances, as another way of giving you a breathing space while you gather your thoughts. But if it is used too often it becomes irritating to the audience, and of course it makes you sound long-winded. Clichés, also, might occasionally be of use – they can help you to keep talking while you consider how to express your next statement. But they should be used sparingly, otherwise you will begin to sound as though you cannot think of anything original to say.

Tips on Speaking Clearly

- Make notes of what you want to say, including particular words and phrases that might clarify your points.

- Go over those notes before you begin to speak so that you have a good idea of what you are going to say and how you are going to say it.

- Have your notes with you when you speak to help you in case you are stuck.

- Speak slowly and in a clear voice.

- Do not 'waffle'; you should be brief and to the point, as you are when writing.

- When involved in a conversation, confirm at particular points that you have understood what the other person has said so far. And do not pretend to understand something you do not.

- Indicate by your tone of voice the impression you are trying to convey – apologetic, conciliatory, firm, enthusiastic.

- Always be polite – even if the other person is rude, do not allow yourself to be drawn into a slanging match.

- Pause at appropriate moments in order to break up what you are saying and give your audience an opportunity to ask questions.

CHAPTER 6
Techniques for different occasions

In Chapter 5 we discussed general points of style which could be applied to most situations. Certain types of communication, however, cause particular problems and therefore warrant special attention. These are:

- requests
- sales letters
- meetings
- complaints
- complex problems
- reports
- presentations

In this chapter we will look at these categories in more detail, and see what special points of style and technique arise when dealing with them.

Making Requests

In Chapter 5 we saw that the tone of your document will depend on your relationship with your audience. If you are making a request, for example, then your success depends very much on how your audience reacts, and your communication needs to reflect that. You need to adopt a tone that indicates that you appreciate that the person you are addressing can refuse or agree to your request.

This does not mean that you should be obsequious. The memo below is *not* a good example of how to get what you want.

To: Mary Pearson
From: Norman Jackson
Date: 14 May 20XX

As you know I have the deepest respect for you as a manager, and particularly for your sense of fairness. I am sure therefore that you will give the request I am about to make every consideration.

I believe I have worked hard during the past year, and in particular that I have achieved the goals you kindly set me when I first started in your department. Indeed, you have been good enough to compliment me on my progress on several occasions, for which I am very grateful – it is always helpful to receive encouragement from one's manager, especially one as busy as you are.

Being busy, you are probably not aware that it is 18 months since my salary was last reviewed. Perhaps I should have mentioned it before, but I did not want to bother you and to be honest, I enjoy working in your department so much that I had almost forgotten myself how long it was.

In view of all this, I would be extremely grateful if you could consider raising my salary. I know I can rely on you to decide on a fair figure, given all the circumstances.

This is too sycophantic and full of flattery, and sounds false. Mary Pearson is more likely to refuse a request expressed in this way.

The other point to remember when making a request is to build up to it gradually. Give the background and the reasons for the request first, rather than coming straight out with it. In that way you prepare your audience, and get them thinking more favourably about the request. If you ask first and then give your reasons, the audience might sub-consciously – or consciously – reject the request before finding out the background. Look at the memo below and you will see the problem.

To: Mary Pearson
From: Norman Jameson
Date: 14 May 20XX

I would like to discuss an increase in my salary commensurate with my progress since joining your department and the level of others on my grade.

As you may know, it is now 18 months since I started in the department. I enjoy working here very much, and I believe that I have worked hard since I joined, and in particular that I have achieved the goals you set me when I first came here. Indeed, you have commented favourably on my progress on several occasions.

However, in that 18 months I have not had a salary review, with the result that my pay is beginning to fall behind that of people on a similar grade in other departments.

As you can see, this version starts off too abruptly – the first paragraph comes over almost as a demand rather than a request.

Now look at the version below.

To: Mary Pearson
From: Norman Jameson
Date: 14 May 20XX

As you may know, it is now 18 months since I started in the department. I enjoy working here very much, and I believe that I have worked hard since I joined, and in particular that I have achieved the goals you set me when I first came here. Indeed, you have commented favourably on my progress on several occasions.

However, in that eighteen months I have not had a salary review, with the result that my pay is beginning to fall behind that of people on a similar grade in other departments.

I wonder therefore whether we could discuss an increase in my salary commensurate with my progress since joining your department and the level of others on my grade.

This is friendly and respectful in tone, without being obsequious. It also builds up to the request, arguing Norman Jameson's case for a salary review before actually asking for it.

EXERCISE 16

You have received information about a course that will be of benefit in your personal professional development. You would like to attend, but it is a week-long residential course and the fee is £1,500. You have spoken to your manager, who is in favour of you attending, but who says that the departmental director must agree. Write a memo or e-mail to the director asking whether you can have the time off to attend the course, and whether the organisation will pay the course fee.

Tips for Making and Answering Requests

- When making a request, be friendly and courteous.
- Give the background to your request or your reasons for making it first, and build up to the request itself.
- When agreeing to a request, do so early in the document or conversation.
- When refusing a request, give your reasons first, then your refusal.
- Do so politely and offer some kind of consolation or hope if possible.

Answering Requests

When you are answering a request you are in a totally different position – you are in control of the situation. But this does not mean that you can be rude or dismissive. You owe it to the other person to be polite.

The style of your response will depend on whether you are agreeing to it or refusing it; each calls for a different approach. The rule of thumb is:

- Say 'yes' quickly, say 'no' slowly.

Agreeing to a request

If you agree with the request, then you should say so immediately. Your aim is always to make a good impression, and to do so as soon as possible. Agreeing to the request should make you very popular, so do it at the start – preferably in the first paragraph, but certainly no later than the second. If there are any strings attached to your agreement, they should come later rather than diluting the good first impression.

The effect of giving the good news immediately will be wasted, however, if you are grudging or high-handed about it. If you sound as though you are doing the other person a great favour, or are acceding to the request grudgingly, you will make quite the wrong impression. Try to sound as though you are *pleased* to be able to agree.

The following letter shows how these guidelines can be put into practice.

MORGAN & MCCARTHY LTD
235 Southampton Row
London WC1D 4KJ
Tel. 020 7245 7864   Fax 020 7245 0973

21 January 20XX

Our Ref. JDL/KM/987432

Mr Patrick Ekwem
Managing Director
Ekwem Enterprises
P.O. Box 13457
Lagos
Nigeria

Dear Mr Ekwem

I have considered your request, made in your letter of 6 January, for an increase in your discount. Your arguments are extremely persuasive, and I am delighted to be able to agree to your request. All future orders will be supplied at 45 per cent discount.

I hope this will be the beginning of an even more fruitful relationship between our two companies. As you say, you have steadily increased your turnover with us over the years, and I am sure that the extra discount will give you the incentive to increase it still more.

Of course you will appreciate that we need a high level of turnover to justify this increased discount, and if your business with us were to fall below its present level, we would have to look at the discount again. However, with the expansion you foresee in the Nigerian market this seems highly unlikely, and I am sure that we will see your turnover continue to rise.

Yours sincerely

John Lamont
Export Manager

John Lamont tells Patrick Ekwem almost immediately that his request for an increase in discount has been granted. He does so gracefully, making it sound as though he is pleased to be able to agree. He has to make a proviso, but he leaves it to the end and takes the sting out of it quite successfully.

Refusing a request

Refusing a request calls for the opposite approach to the one you would adopt if you were agreeing to it. Build up to the refusal gradually. Express an understanding of the other person's problem, explain the lengths you have gone to to find a way of solving it, give the reasons for your refusal, and *then* say 'no'. As with agreeing, your aim is to make as good an impression as possible. Building up to your refusal gives you a chance to get the other person at least to understand your position before the disappointment of being turned down.

Once again, this impression can be spoiled if your tone is wrong. Do not think, just because you are in control when refusing a request, that you can be insulting or impolite. Always be courteous when turning someone down. Not only is it good manners, it is also in your own interests. If you are refusing a subordinate, it makes sense to try to lessen the disappointment and not to demotivate him or her. And if it is a member of the public or a client, you have your organisation's image to consider.

For the same reason, see whether you can somehow soften the blow by offering some hope for the future, no matter how tenuous. You could just say, 'I will get back to you if the situation changes' or 'I will keep your letter on file' or you could offer something specific for the other person to aim for.

The letter below is one that John Lamont might have written to refuse Patrick Ekwem's request for an increase in discount.

MORGAN & MCCARTHY LTD
235 Southampton Row
London WC1D 4KJ
Tel. 020 7245 7864   Fax 020 7245 0973

21 January 20XX

Our Ref. JDL/KM/987432

Mr Patrick Ekwem
Managing Director
Ekwem Enterprises
P.O. Box 13457
Lagos
Nigeria

Dear Mr Ekwem

Thank you for your letter of 6 January. I take your point about the increase in your turnover with us recently. We are very grateful for your support over the years.

Because of this support, and the good relations between our two companies, I have considered your request carefully, and have looked at it from every angle. I have also consulted my colleagues on the Board of Directors.

Our problem is that there are a number of other customers, in Nigeria and elsewhere, who do more business with us than you do, and who receive the same discount. I am sure you will appreciate that it would not be fair to them if we were to increase your discount without doing the same for them – and increasing everyone's discount would be uneconomic.

I am afraid, therefore, that we cannot agree to your request at present. However, I do not want to be inflexible, and would be very willing to reconsider the position if you were able to increase your turnover a little more. If, therefore, you were to achieve a turnover of £300,000 this year, I would be happy to grant you the discount you ask for. It would then remain at 45 per cent for as long as your turnover was at that level.

Yours sincerely

John Lamont
Export Manager

As you can see, he builds up to the refusal gradually; he is polite, even regretful at having to say 'no', and he offers him hope in the form of something to aim for – if he increases his turnover to a certain level, he will be granted the extra discount.

EXERCISE 17

Imagine that you are the departmental director to whom you addressed your request to attend a course in Exercise 16. Write a reply refusing the request on the grounds that, although there might be some benefit to the organisation, it is likely to be minimal, and would not justify the cost.

Writing Sales Letters

Sales or promotional letters resemble advertisements, and when writing them you should be thinking like an advertiser. Adopt an enthusiastic tone and choose positive words. You should also pay particular attention to the order in which you present your case.

Enthusiasm is important; if you are not enthusiastic about your product or service, how can you expect your readers to be? So although you should not be so enthusiastic that you mislead your readers, you do need to adopt a positive, upbeat tone.

Similarly, you should use positive words. If you are writing about a problem the customer might have, to which you have the solution, then you can use words with a negative connotation, but otherwise avoid them, and do not use negative words when referring directly to your reader. So you could say, 'Does your office become messy and littered because there is no one with direct responsibility for cleaning it?' But you would put your reader off if you said, 'I will take complete responsibility for your messy and littered office.' In the first sentence you are only asking if the reader's office is messy. In the second, you are implying that it *is* messy.

Look at the following letter.

MILTON FLORISTS
15 Union Street, Milton, MN1 2OP
Tel. 01231 987234

30 May 20XX

Dear Client

Do you sometimes feel that your offices could do with a little brightening up? Does your reception area look bright and welcoming or drab and discouraging? Do your pot plants tend to wilt and wither because everyone is too busy to care for them properly?

Bright, cheerful premises can make all the difference to an organisation. When clients and visitors come to your office, a colourful floral display in reception will make them feel welcome, and will enhance your corporate image. And plants and flowers, by making offices attractive places to work in, can also improve the morale of staff.

I can help you make your office a happy, welcoming place for staff and visitors alike. My service to businesses – the only one of its kind in Milton – includes:

- a full discussion of your needs
- a survey of the premises to suggest particular plants and flowers for particular locations
- the supply of all plants and flowers
- regular care of plants, from feeding and watering to replacement when necessary
- replacement of all flower arrangements on a regular basis

Moreover, I can tailor the service to suit your requirements and your budget.

Because I am a fully qualified horticulturalist and I always deal with my business clients personally, you can be sure of an expert, professional service. I would be delighted to come and discuss your needs, and to show you how I could help you. Please phone me at any time.

Yours sincerely

Pam Silverman

You can see that all the words and images associated with Pam Silverman's service are positive – a good corporate image, a pleasing place to work, good staff morale, a complete service. The negative images are all associated with the lack of this service – and none of them is applied directly to the client.

Before you write a sales letter, however, you must be sure that you know who your message is aimed at and what benefits you are offering.

What market are you aiming at?

To be effective, a sales letter should be aimed at a specific market. Many people seem to think that they can write an all-purpose letter that will appeal to a wide range of customers. This is very seldom the case. If you have a product or service that you think will appeal to more than one group of people, then you would be better off writing more than one version of your sales letter.

The reason is that you might need to emphasise different aspects of a product or service to appeal to different audiences. The letter above, for example, is aimed at business people, so Pam writes about a service geared to their needs. A letter to members of the public, or to people planning a wedding, would have quite a different emphasis.

Not only will the emphasis of your message depend on your audience, so will your language, your tone and the imagery you use. If you are selling an interior design service to very up-market clients, you will use language that is appropriate; you will talk about decor, style, ambience, quality. On the other hand, if you are writing about the opening of a new bargain store, you will talk about special offers, low prices, bargains, free gifts.

So before you start writing, decide exactly who your message is aimed at, and choose an approach and language suited to that market.

What benefits are you offering?

Readers of sales or promotional letters are not interested in you, nor in your organisation. They are not even particularly interested in what you are selling *per se*. What they want to know is what you can do for them – what benefits you can offer them.

The benefits might vary according to the audience. Pam Silverman's letter to businesses points to several advantages she can offer: an attractive office environment, a good company image, a service tailored to the company's needs and budget, the only service of its kind in town. If she were writing to personal clients, she would offer different benefits: the beauty of flowers as a gift, for example, special rates for weddings and big occasions, a same-day delivery service. It is therefore important to decide on the market you are aiming at, and then to think of all the benefits you can offer that market.

Unique Selling Propositions and Emotional Buying Triggers
These are two concepts in advertising that can be useful when writing sales letters.

- **A unique selling proposition (USP)** is simply jargon for something that makes your product or service unique, something you have that your competitors do not. In the case of Pam Silverman's florist's shop, it is the fact that she will not only supply flowers and plants to businesses, but also ensure that they are cared for and replaced from time to time. It is not essential to have a USP, but if you do have one, then make a point of it in your letter. Do not, however, try too hard. There may be a feature of your product or service that is unique to you, but which is relatively unimportant; if you place too much emphasis on such a feature it could be counterproductive. So if, for example, you are promoting a range of paints, the fact that you have one more colour in your range than your competitor's could be seen as a USP, but it is unlikely to persuade your readers to buy your paints rather than theirs.

- **Emotional buying triggers** are appeals to your readers' emotions and instincts. The need to be liked, to project the 'right' image, to achieve, to feel secure, to be an individual – all of these can trigger a positive response if they are given the right stimulus. But, as with USPs, they should not be forced.

As you think of the benefits, make a list and then try to put them in order of importance. You need not be too precise – a rough order will do. But do get them in order so that when you come to write your letter, you know which are the most important benefits, the ones that need to be emphasised.

AIDA and the four Ps

When you have decided on your market and the benefits you offer, you need to ensure that you present your letter in a way that is most likely to achieve a positive response. There are two ways of presenting a sales letter: AIDA and the four Ps.

- **AIDA** comes directly from advertising, and is a way of remembering the order in which you should present your case. The letters stand for:
  - Attention
  - Interest
  - Desire
  - Action

In other words you should first aim to attract your readers' attention. Then you must hold their interest. Next you need to convert that interest into a desire for your product or service. And finally you should indicate what action you want them to take.

- The **four Ps** are:
  - Promise
  - Picture
  - Proof
  - Push

  With this approach, you promise the reader certain benefits. You create a picture showing how he or she will gain those benefits, prove that you can deliver them, and then provide a 'push' to action. Unlike AIDA, it is not essential to stick to this order, although the 'push' should usually come last.

The two formulae are not mutually exclusive; some of the best sales letters conform to both. Pam Silverman's letter, for example, is written to the AIDA formula. The first paragraph, with its questions, attracts the attention of the target audience. The next holds their interest, as it shows how flowers and plants can make a difference to an office. The details of the service create a desire for it, and the last paragraph prompts the client to action. It also conforms to the four Ps. It paints a picture of how Pam's service could change the client's organisation. It promises that it can benefit the client. It proves that Pam can deliver the benefit by mentioning her qualifications and personal service. And it gives a 'push' towards action.

EXERCISE 18

Look again at the letter you wrote in Exercise 13. Make any changes you think might be necessary to turn it into an effective promotional letter.

Conducting Meetings

Most of us have been to meetings that seem to go on for ever, often without any firm conclusions having been reached. This is usually because of one or more of the following problems:

- There is no clear agenda.
- The meeting is inefficiently chaired.
- People wander off the point.
- The discussion goes round in circles, without any clear decisions being made.

Few people enjoy meetings for their own sake, but they are often the best way of communicating with colleagues and others, and of making decisions that require the involvement of several people – provided they are efficiently run. And this requires advance preparation, as well as clear guidelines as to how the meeting is to be conducted.

Efficient Meetings

These are the characteristics of an efficient meeting.

- The agenda makes it clear what is to be discussed, and which items require a decision.
- Participants are notified of the meeting, the venue and the agenda in good time.
- Any papers that might be referred to are circulated in advance to enable participants to come prepared.
- Someone is delegated to take the minutes.
- Everyone is given a chance to put their point of view before any decisions are made.
- Participants do not stray off the point.
- The discussion does not become bogged down in unnecessary detail.
- Clear decisions are made.
- It does not go on too long. Two hours is generally regarded as the maximum length; after that people's concentration is likely to be affected.
- Clear minutes are taken and distributed soon after the meeting.

Arranging a meeting

Although a small, informal exchange of views might not require very much preparation, more formal meetings, at which important decisions are to be made, should be arranged with care. The first thing you need to do is to ensure that everyone involved is notified *in writing* (which includes e-mail). Even if you have already contacted them by telephone, you should confirm the details in writing. The notification should include the following information:

- the purpose of the meeting
- the date

- the time
- the venue (and how to reach it if any of the participants might not know where it is)

There should also be an agenda, either as part of the notification or as a separate attachment. This agenda should be clearly expressed and decision-driven, so that everyone knows what is to be discussed and what outcome is expected for each item. For example, people attending a meeting with the following agenda would not have very much idea what is expected of them.

MANAGEMENT MEETING, 12 OCTOBER 20XX
AGENDA

1. Minutes of the last meeting

2. Matters arising

3. Finance

4. Managers' conference

5. Expenses

6. Staff attitudes to recent organisational changes

7. Date of the next meeting

How much clearer it would be if it were expressed like the following.

MANAGEMENT MEETING, 12 OCTOBER 20XX
AGENDA

1. To agree the minutes of the last meeting

2. To consider matters arising

3. To receive a financial report

4. To decide on arrangements for the managers' conference

5. To review the policy on payment of expenses

6. To set up a group to conduct a survey of staff attitudes to recent organisational changes

7. To decide the date of the next meeting

Everyone would then be clear about what was expected of them under each item. And in order to ensure that the meeting does not overrun, some people will put a time limit on each item on the agenda. However, such a system needs to be flexibly operated – it may be that a particular item, which appears uncontroversial when you are planning the meeting, requires rather more discussion that you anticipated. It would be foolish to stifle genuine – and useful – discussion just for the sake of an arbitrary time limit.

Any discussion papers, reports or other documents that are likely to be referred to at the meeting should be circulated in advance, preferably with the agenda. This will enable participants to read them and make a note of any questions or points they want to raise, so that they come to the meeting prepared, rather than either having to read the background to the discussion during the meeting (which will prevent them from participating fully in the debate) or having to have the main points explained to them (which will waste time). With the above agenda, for example, the organiser of the meeting should circulate the financial report, the policy on the payment of expenses, and perhaps details of any previous discussions about the managers' conference.

EXERCISE 19

You have been asked to set up a meeting to discuss arrangements for the staff Christmas party in your organisation. Draft a memo or e-mail to send to all those who should be involved, notifying them of the meeting and including an agenda.

Chairing a meeting

Chairing a meeting requires tact and firmness. It is the chair's responsibility to ensure that the meeting does not descend into a slanging match between people with different views, but that participants respect each other's opinions, even when they disagree with them. He or she must also give everyone present a chance to speak, so that the meeting is not dominated by a vocal minority. Participants must also not be allowed to 'waffle' or to stray from the agenda. And if a report or other paper has been circulated in advance, the chair must prevent its author wasting time by reading it out again at the meeting. The aim should be for other participants to raise questions and discussion points arising out of the paper, not for the author to repeat orally what is already available in writing.

The meeting should generally follow the order of the agenda, unless there is a good reason not to. And the person in the chair needs to ensure that, as each item comes up, only matters relating to it are discussed. It is all too easy for people to stray from the subject, perhaps so that they can introduce their particular hobby horse. The chair must be very firm in preventing that from happening, otherwise the meeting can degenerate into a free-for-all.

There is also a tendency for items to be allowed to run into each other; the problem here is that no one is quite sure when discussion of a particular item has ended and a new one has begun, which could lead to people going back to previous items and reopening discussions that others thought were closed. The chair must therefore make it clear when the meeting has come to the end of each item, usually by using one of the following devices:

- Calling for a vote. Of course, if no decision is required, then there will be no vote. And even if a decision is required, if it is obvious that there is a consensus among participants, then a vote may not be necessary. But if there is clearly some disagreement, or if the issue is particularly important, then the chair should call for a vote. Once the vote is taken, that item should not be discussed again.

- Summarising the outcome of the discussion. If no vote has been taken, it can be useful to provide a brief summary. But it should be a summary of the *outcome*, not of what was actually said and by whom. Again, once the chair has summarised what was decided, he or she should not allow that item to be revisited.
- Saying firmly something like, 'I think we have said everything that needs to be said on that subject. Can we move on to the next item?'

It is also the chair's responsibility to ensure that clear decisions are made when necessary (and obviously a decision-driven agenda will help in this).

Speaking at a meeting

Everyone attending a meeting has a responsibility to ensure that it goes smoothly, not just the person in the chair. The basic rules of business communication apply here, just as they do in other circumstances: when you speak you should be brief, clear and direct. You should also avoid being rude. But there are other rules that are particular to meetings.

- Before the meeting, you should read any papers that have been circulated and make a note of any points you particularly want to raise.
- You should bring any papers to the meeting so that, if necessary, you can refer to them.
- You should listen to what the other participants say and respect their views, even if you disagree with them.
- When expressing disagreement, you should do so politely.
- You should not interrupt someone while they are speaking. The only person who should do that is the chair, and only if the person is straying from the subject or preventing others from having their say. If you want to speak while someone else is doing so, raise your hand in a slight gesture to attract the chair's attention; they should then call on you to speak as soon as it is feasible.
- Being brief means that you should not carry on talking unnecessarily – say what you want to say, bearing in mind all the techniques of brevity we have already discussed, and then allow someone else to speak.
- Do not stray from the subject under discussion.
- Once a decision has been reached, you should not try to reopen the discussion, even if you disagree with what has been decided. You can, if necessary, ask for it to be discussed again at a future meeting, but until then you will have to live with the decision that has been made.

Writing minutes

Although, as with most business communications, there is a degree of flexibility in the way minutes are presented, there is a general style to which you should adhere. The first rule is that minutes should follow the order of the agenda. The second is that there should be a heading for each item. It is also important to include the date of the meeting so that anyone wanting to refer to them later will know which meeting they refer to, and to indicate who was present in case any queries arise later.

Minutes should summarise the main points raised at the meeting and indicate what decisions were made. They should not be a blow-by-blow account of what was said and by whom. Indeed, apart from indicating who introduced particular papers or who was asked to undertake a specific task, it is very often not necessary to mention individuals at all. Even when a vote is taken, it is usual simply to give the numbers for and against rather than indicating how everyone voted. Some organisations prefer (or are even required) to minute how each participant voted in the interests of openness, particularly those whose members are elected representatives, such as local government. Moreover, it may occasionally happen that someone who disagrees strongly with a decision asks for their disagreement to be minuted, but otherwise it is unusual to say how individuals reacted.

Below is how the minutes of the management meeting whose agenda is shown above might appear, bearing in mind these guidelines.

Minutes of the Management Meeting held on 12 October 20XX

Present: Mary King (Chair), Patrick Baptiste, Stephen Martinson, Belinda Snow, Farida Aftab, Keith Sturgess, James Watson

1. *Minutes of the last meeting*. These were agreed as a true record.
2. *Matters arising*.
    a. *Item 4*. PB reported that the redundancy policy had been to the unions for consultation as agreed, and he was still waiting for their response.
3. *Financial report*. This had previously been circulated and is attached. BS explained that, since it was produced, some long-standing debts to the organisation had been settled, and the cash-flow situation was therefore more positive than the figures suggested. There was some discussion about the forecast for the end of the year, but it was agreed that the organisation's financial situation looked very healthy.
4. *Arrangements for the managers' conference*. The following arrangements were decided:
    a. *Venue*. Several venues were suggested, but it was finally agreed that the Lockwood Hotel provided the best facilities.
    b. *Date*. Friday, 2 December.
    c. *Format*. After considerable discussion, it was agreed that the conference should focus on our key priorities for the coming year, rather than involving a department-by-department analysis of performance. A list of these priorities and the senior managers who have agreed to make presentations on them is attached. Each presentation is to last one hour (including questions).
5. *Policy on payment of expenses*. This policy was reviewed. It was decided, by six votes to one, that no change should be made to the current policy, nor to the amounts that can be claimed. JW asked to have it minuted that he did not agree with this decision: he felt that the amounts should be increased in line with the retail price index.
6. *Survey of staff attitudes to recent organisational changes*. As previously agreed, a group is to be set up to conduct this survey and report back to a future meeting. This group will comprise: MK, SM and FA.
7. *Date of the next meeting*. 15 November 20XX

EXERCISE 20

If you are working in a group, role-play a short meeting to discuss the Christmas party, based on the agenda you drafted in Exercise 19 (or on the example given in the answer to that exercise). Then write up the minutes of that meeting. If you are working on your own, write your own minutes of a meeting you have recently attended.

Making Complaints

When you are complaining about something, do not become aggressive or abusive, especially if it is your first communication. The action – or lack of action – about which you are complaining could well be the result of a genuine error or misunderstanding. We all make mistakes, and it is only common courtesy to give the other person the benefit of the doubt. As we have seen, emotion has no place in business communications; not only is it good manners to be polite and unemotional, it will probably be in your own long-term interests. An aggressive approach might get results, but it could easily make the other person defensive and uncooperative, and it could be at the expense of your long-term business relationship. As always, put yourself in your audience's shoes. How would you react if you received a letter like the following?

C. J. DOBSON PLUMBER

45 King Street
Brownchurch
BC2 1DE
Tel. 01987 654321

3 September 20XX

The Manager
National Midland Bank
5 High Street
Brownchurch
BC1 2FG

Dear Sir/Madam

Are you trying to bankrupt me? Don't you get enough out of me legally without trying to cheat me as well?

For the last three months my statements have shown interest charges for an overdraft, together with a 'service charge' of £50 and 'transaction charges' of varying amounts. I was overdrawn by £1,000 for a short period in May, so I expected to pay a small amount of interest in June, and perhaps a small charge. But I did not expect to be penalised for the next three months. Do you realise that you have taken a total of £300 of my money? And for all I know my next statement will show another amount deducted.

This is not the kind of treatment I expect from my 'friendly High Street bank'. You will please credit my account with the excess you have taken, plus interest, immediately. If I do not receive a corrected statement within a week, I shall take my account elsewhere and report you to the Office of Fair Trading.

Yours faithfully

Charles Dobson

You would hopefully correct the error, but you would not feel very well disposed towards the writer – Charles Dobson would have soured his relationship with an important person in the success of his business.

The Four-stage Approach to Complaining

1 Write a friendly letter, e-mail or memo, or make a friendly call, explaining the nature of your complaint and the action you would like taken.

2 If you do not receive a reply, or no action is taken, contact the organisation or person again, still in a friendly way, but take a slightly firmer line.

3 If you still do not receive satisfaction, drop the friendly tone but remain polite.

4 Finally (and this stage should always be in writing), while remaining polite, threaten some kind of action – withholding payment, reporting your correspondent to the authorities, legal action, whatever seems appropriate to the nature of the complaint.

It is important to keep a record of the date on which you took each action and the outcome, if any, even if you are phoning rather than writing. In that way you can refer back to each stage if necessary.

Before you start writing, you should have two things clear in your mind:

- What precisely are you complaining about?
- What do you want done about it?

It is no use complaining in a general way – about 'poor' service, for example, or 'shoddy' workmanship or 'late' delivery – unless you have specific details to quote. The other person can only take corrective action if he or she knows *precisely* where things have gone wrong.

Similarly, they can do little more than apologise if you do not say what corrective action you want taken. This action may simply be to improve the service, workmanship or delivery you receive, but even then you should try to be specific. What level of service do you expect? What do you consider a satisfactory delivery time? And of course, many complaints require more specific action – to issue a credit note, to replace faulty goods, or to compensate you for financial loss.

With the answers to these questions, you should be able to prepare your complaint, which should be in three parts:

- a polite introduction, perhaps pointing out the good relationship you have enjoyed with the other person or organisation so far
- the specific details of your complaint
- a request for corrective action

Overleaf is a letter based on this format.

C. J. DOBSON PLUMBER
45 King Street
Brownchurch
BC2 1DE
Tel. 01987 654321

3 September 20XX

Mr Gordon Marshall
Manager
National Midland Bank
5 High Street
Brownchurch
BC1 2FG

Dear Mr Marshall

ACCOUNT NO. 43876653

As you know, I have been a customer of your bank for many years, and I have always found you and your staff friendly and efficient. I hope, therefore, that you will be able to correct what I assume is an error in your computer systems.

In May I was overdrawn by £1,000 for a short period, owing to an unexpected repair to my van. I know that I should have cleared the overdraft with you, but as I say, the bill was unforseen. I therefore expected to have to pay interest on that amount, as well as a charge for becoming overdrawn without prior clearance. The relevant amounts were shown on my June statement, and I thought that was the end of it.

However, I have had interest, a service charge and transaction charges deducted in July and August as well, with the result that I have paid a total of £300. I am sure this cannot be correct, and I can only assume that your computer is automatically deducting these charges on the assumption that I am still overdrawn.

I would be grateful, therefore, if you would look into the matter and credit my account with the excess that has been deducted, plus any interest that might have accrued.

I look forward to receiving an amended statement shortly.

Yours sincerely

Charles Dobson

This is friendly and clear, and should achieve Charles Dobson's objective as well as the previous example, while keeping the relationship with his bank manager on a friendly basis.

EXERCISE 21

You are refurbishing your office and have ordered 30 workstations and chairs. You only receive 28 of each, and of these 12 are not the style you ordered. Prepare notes for a telephone call complaining to the supplier.

Answering Complaints

How can you turn a complaining customer into a satisfied one? It is not too difficult. The first thing the person wants is to be reassured that you take the complaint seriously. Too many so-called customer service departments, even (or perhaps especially) in large companies, try to fob complainers off with what are quite obviously standard letters which do not address the nature of their complaints at all. One is left with the impression that they have no interest in correcting any underlying fault in their system.

Beyond that, what is needed is a friendly approach, a conciliatory attitude, and a willingness to take any action that may be necessary if you are at fault. Even if you are rejecting the complaint, it is possible to do so without causing offence.

The answer to a complaint can be divided into two or three parts, depending on whether you are accepting or rejecting it:

- the apology if you accept the complaint, or an expression of regret or concern if you reject it
- the explanation
- the remedy if you accept the complaint

The apology or expression of concern

The best way to keep your customer happy is to express your concern, whatever the outcome. So even if you are rejecting the complaint, try to find something to express concern about. Here are a few examples of what you might say:

- I was very concerned to hear that you are dissatisfied with our service.
- I am very sorry if our terms of trade were not clear, but if you look at item 12 ...
- I am sorry if I did not make myself clear on the telephone.
- I am sorry if you misunderstood the terms of our agreement.

Nobody likes to be told that they are wrong, even if they know that they are – least of all customers. They might misunderstand or misinterpret things, but they are not wrong.

But do not take this 'apology' too far. You can apologise for not making yourself clear, but do not actually say that you are wrong just to be polite. It could set an awkward precedent and cause a great many problems. If you apologise for a late delivery, for example, when it was the customer's fault that the delivery was late, then you could lay yourself open to a claim for compensation. Taking another example, if you apologise for poor service, then the customer will expect an improvement. But if you did everything possible to help him or her, you will not be able to make any improvements and the customer is likely to be disappointed again. Express concern about any dissatisfaction, explain the situation fully, apologise for any misunderstanding and be friendly, but state quite clearly that you believe you are right.

If, on the other hand, you are wrong, you should admit it and apologise. You can even make the other person feel that he or she has done you a favour by expressing your thanks. Here are some examples:

- We always welcome our customers' views on our service, as it is only through this feedback that we can improve. I am only sorry that we have treated you so badly.
- Thank you for raising the matter with me. Your letter has highlighted a fault in our system which we are now able to correct. I do apologise, however, for the inconvenience you have been caused.

If you use expressions like these, you will show that you are taking the complaint seriously, and that you will not only take corrective action in respect of the person's actual complaint, but also rectify any faults in your system. Note, too, that in the latter case the writer apologises for '*the* inconvenience you have been caused', not '*any* inconvenience', which is a phrase one sees far too often. There is no question about whether the complainant has been caused any inconvenience. The very fact that he or she has had to write or telephone is in itself an inconvenience.

So if you have to apologise, do so unreservedly. Too often people in business try to hide behind bland, formal expressions when apologising, as if trying to avoid responsibility. 'We regret any inconvenience caused' is just such an expression. It seems to imply:

- that the writer does not believe that you have really been inconvenienced
- that even if you have, it is not really anyone's fault, and is a cause for regret rather than an apology
- that if it is anyone's responsibility, it is the company's ('we') rather than the individual's ('I')

The other way in which people try to avoid responsibility is by making excuses. They give details of how their supplier has let them down, or explain at great length how short-staffed they are, or blame the whole thing on someone who has now left the organisation, and in the process they seem to forget to apologise.

A great many business people still react to complaints like this, but would complain bitterly if they were subjected to the same treatment. On the other hand, most of us would feel much better disposed towards someone who accepted responsibility, apologised and took corrective action than towards someone who tried to make excuses and corrected the error grudgingly and without apology. By all means explain the circumstances behind the error (see below), but do so briefly, and do not think that your explanation is a substitute for an apology.

The explanation

When you have apologised, you should give some explanation of the facts of the case. If you accept the complaint, then it is a good idea to give some explanation of what went wrong. But do not let your explanation get in the way of your apology: the apology comes first, so that the explanation does not look like an excuse. You should also not go into too much detail. By all means say that you were let down by your supplier, or that your system for dealing with orders was at fault, but then leave it at that. What your complainant wants is an apology and a remedy; the explanation may make them more understanding, and make them feel that you take the complaint seriously, but only if you keep it brief.

If you are rejecting the complaint, your explanation needs to be longer. You have to try to convince the complainant that your rejection is justified, much as you do when rejecting a request, and you can only do that if you go into a certain amount of detail.

Rejecting a Complaint

- Be polite.

- Express regret or concern that the person has had to contact you.

- Give the impression in your explanation that you have investigated the complaint fully, no matter how trivial it really is.

- Give all the facts as you understand them, particularly where your understanding differs from that of your correspondent.

- If there are any other people who can back up your version of events, then say who they are.

Below is an example of a letter rejecting a complaint, putting the techniques discussed above into effect.

CARLTON & DAVIES
BUILDING CONTRACTORS
24 Queen Street, Morganston, MG2 3HI
Tel. 01356 789012

Our ref. MD/KR/19876

8 February 20XX

Mr J.P. Stephenson
5 Brooms Close
Morganston
MG4 9KN

Dear Mr Stephenson

I was very concerned to see from your letter of 31 January that you are not satisfied with our response to your request for repairs to be made to your roof.

On receipt of your letter, I conducted a thorough investigation of all the circumstances of the job. I spoke to our telephonist, our Works Manager and the men who carried out the work.

What happened, as I understand it, is that you telephoned us on 15 January to say that there was a leak in your roof, and that the rain was coming in. Because of the storms, we had a great many emergency calls that day, and you were told by the telephonist that someone would call as soon as possible. She also, I believe, advised you on short-term measures you could take to alleviate the problem. You confirmed that you would be at home for the rest of the day.

Our workmen did in fact call later – at about eight o'clock, according to their worksheet – but you were not at home. You say that they should have made the necessary repairs in your absence but unfortunately, in order to do so, they needed access to the house. I believe that they left a note to that effect. They did, however, call again next day, when you were in. As you say, the repair they made then was only temporary, but the men concerned tell me that they did point that out at the time. I am very sorry if you misunderstood them. The reason ▶

for the temporary repair was that we were still receiving emergency calls. To make a permanent repair would have taken several hours, and they were certain that their temporary job would hold until they were able to return and finish it – as in fact it did.

They returned a week later to complete the job. You say that you should not have had to wait that long, but as I have said, we had a great many emergencies to deal with. It was therefore not possible to come back any sooner, and the temporary repair did ensure that in the meantime you did not suffer any inconvenience.

I agree that our service was not as fast as we would normally like it to be, but I am sure you will appreciate that the situation was not normal. I do believe that under the circumstances we did everything possible to accommodate you. I am afraid therefore that we cannot agree to waive our charge for the repair.

Yours sincerely

Martin Davies
Director

The remedy

If you accept the complaint, then in the final part of your letter (before you sign off, perhaps with another brief apology) you should outline how you intend to remedy the situation. This could simply involve changes to your systems or your way of doing things so that the same mistake does not happen again. Or it could take a more concrete form, such as giving the complainant a credit note, cancelling an invoice, or paying some form of compensation. It all depends on the circumstances.

But remember that goodwill is important in any business relationship. If you have committed an error or inconvenienced a business contact in any way, it is worth a bit of trouble, and even money, to ensure that the goodwill is not lost. So when it comes to a remedy, err on the side of generosity.

Below is a letter accepting a complaint. It includes all the elements we have been talking about, from a graceful and unreserved apology to a brief explanation of what went wrong and then a generous suggestion for remedying the situation.

NEW MODE FASHIONS
5 Thornton Road, Langton LT2 3UV
(01234 987654

12 July 20XX

Mrs J. Wilson
Hilton & Co.
46 Kilsey Street
Osberton
OS1 2TU

Dear Mrs Wilson

I was extremely sorry to see from your letter of 5 July that your special order of 20 June was delivered late. I am grateful to you, however, for giving me such full details of the order and delivery, as it has enabled me to trace and correct a fault in our order processing system.

What apparently happened was that the order was held back because the computer showed a query on your account. By the time we discovered that the query was a computer error, the consignment was late. We have now corrected the error, and have instituted a system for informing customers immediately if there is likely to be any delay in the despatch of their orders.

This means that this should not happen again, but I realise that it does not solve your immediate problem, which is that your customer has cancelled her order. I would therefore like to make the following two suggestions:

1. We will cancel your invoice for the garments, enabling you to give them to your customer free of charge as a means of regaining her goodwill.

2. We will in addition credit you with the full value of the order, to compensate you for the loss of business you have suffered.

I hope that these suggestions meet with your approval, and that you will accept my apologies for the inconvenience you have been caused.

Yours sincerely

Gillian Holding
Managing Director

EXERCISE 22

Look again at Exercise 21. Imagine that you work for the supplier of the office equipment, and you have received the telephone call for which you made notes in that exercise. You have conducted an investigation and find that the company is indeed at fault. Write a letter accepting the complaint.

Clarifying Complex Problems

One of the hardest letters to write is the one designed to sort out a situation where the correspondence has become bogged down in a mass of claims and counter-claims to the extent that the two organisations cannot agree on what the situation is. Every letter, e-mail or telephone call seems to add yet further complexity; it requires a lot of research, a lot of patience, clear thinking and clear writing to unravel it all – and clear writing is absolutely crucial. Make quite sure that there is no ambiguity or vagueness in your letter (and in this situation you should definitely write, not try to resolve the issue over the telephone), because there must be no further misunderstanding to muddy the waters.

The most common situation in which such problems arise is in reconciling accounts, where a plethora of invoices, counter-invoices, credit notes and queries seem to fly back and forth, adding layer upon layer of complexity. But they can also occur when there are disagreements over deliveries, over who is responsible for which aspects of a contract, or over the extent of a company's liability for unsatisfactory service. The letter from Martin Davies above, in which he rejected Mr Stephenson's complaint, is a simple example of this kind of letter.

There are four stages to this task.

1. Assemble *all* the information that is remotely relevant to the situation. This means every invoice, every credit note, every statement, every delivery note, every letter or e-mail received or written, by you or anyone else, any notes of telephone conversations.

2. Go through it all, preferably in chronological order. Make sure that you have a copy of every document referred to in the correspondence (and if it is an accounting query, every invoice or credit note referred to in any statements). If there are any items you do not have, and they cannot be found, make a note. Read everything, several times if necessary, until you fully understand the situation. It can sometimes help to make notes as you go along, but however you do it, make sure that it is all quite clear in your mind.

3. Write your letter, setting out the situation as you now understand it, in a clear and logical sequence. The clearest sequence may be chronological order, but with certain accounting queries it could be numerical order by invoice or the order in which items appear on a statement. Explain how each document mentioned fits (or does not fit) into the picture and give a summary of the situation (in an accounting query, this will be who owes what, but in other circumstances it will be different – for example, with a contractual problem it might be who needs to take action). If your correspondent refers to documents you do not have, ask for copies. If you mention documents (particularly invoices, delivery notes or credit notes) which he or she does not appear to have, enclose copies.

4. Do not give your correspondent a chance to introduce any confusion into the situation. Insist that, if they agree with your analysis, they should take any action you propose, and if they disagree they should indicate precisely what they disagree with and provide documentation to support their case. In other words, ensure that any further correspondence relates to your analysis. And insist that they respond in writing; a telephone call will only provide another opportunity for misunderstanding to arise.

If you follow these four steps, your letter should produce the desired result. But the most important steps are probably the first two. If you do not have all the information in front of you, and if you do not fully understand the situation yourself, then your letter will probably just cloud the issue still further.

Below is a letter showing how this four-stage approach works in practice. It is clear, each document is presented and explained, there is a summary of what Brian Wagstaff believes his company owes, and there is a clear statement of what he expects Wendy Cartwright to do next.

FRANCIS MONK & CO
6 High Street, Midchester, MC1 4GF
Tel. 01324 123456

Wendy Cartwright
Financial Director
Canter Distribution Ltd
5 Jarvis Way
Branston
BT3 7YH

9 March 20XX

Dear Ms Cartwright

Thank you for your letter of 2 March, sent with your February statement. Perhaps if I explain, item by item, what our understanding is of the situation between our two companies, we can resolve this dispute once and for all.

Invoice 14235. This was paid on 25 October with our cheque No. 015943, which was cleared on 10 November. My colleague Henry Thompson asked for the item to be cleared from our statement in his letter of 6 January, but it has not yet been done.

Invoice 14425. This invoice was charged at the wrong discount. On 22 January, Henry Thompson wrote and asked for a credit note to amend the discount. Your colleague Lawrence Davies wrote to him on 5 February to say that instead of issuing a credit note you would cancel the invoice and issue a new one.

Invoice 14457. This is for exactly the same goods as invoice 14425. Since we did not order two consignments, I assume that it was intended to cancel invoice 14425, although nothing to that effect appears on the invoice itself. On 3 February, I e-mailed asking whether this was the case. The only reply I received was an unsigned e-mail on 10 February, saying that the invoice was correct, but with no further explanation.

Invoice 14534. I agree this invoice.

Credit note 10987. This relates to faulty goods received on invoice 14534, and is correct.

Invoice 14768. I agree this invoice.

Invoice 14784. I agree this invoice.

Credit note 11259. There is no mention on this credit note of what it relates to. From the amount, I assume that it is to correct invoice 14425, on which we were given the wrong discount (see above).

Missing from your statement is any reference to our invoice 08976 of 6 February (copy attached), relating to the return of goods. I can confirm that the goods were delivered – our delivery note is signed by Ted Victor.

The correct position, as I see it, is therefore as follows:

Amount due, as per your statement:	£1,862.79
Less invoice 14235, already paid:	(£234.63)
Less invoice 14425, which should have been cancelled:	(£526.46)
Add credit note 11259, which should not have been raised:	£96.23
Less our invoice 08976:	(£186.54)

Actual amount due:	£1,011.39

If you agree with my analysis, I would be grateful if you would send me an amended statement. As soon as I receive it, I shall send you a cheque for the full amount. If you do not agree with my understanding of the position, perhaps you could let me know, in writing, what in particular you disagree with, and let me have details of how your view differs from mine.

Yours sincerely

Brian Wagstaff
Chief Accountant

Writing Reports

A good report is a joy to read – clear, concise, well argued and to the point. It leaves no sign of the effort that has gone into making it like that! Good reports take time and care, however, and require particular skills to compile. We discussed the layout of reports in Chapter 3; here we will be looking at the techniques involved in writing them.

Assembling the facts

Whatever kind of report you are writing, you will be gathering facts. Facts are the basis of any report, and before you even begin to plan one, you should make sure that you have all the relevant facts. And that means *all* the facts. Do not just gather those facts that fit some preconceived idea you may have and ignore everything else. That is dishonest, it invalidates the whole report (which is of no use if it is not objective), and there is a strong chance that someone reading it will know something you have left out.

And do not just select information that seems to be especially relevant and ignore anything that looks less important. Until you start to sift and analyse your facts, you will not know how important each piece of information is.

The trick in writing reports is to make them as short as you can while still including everything that is relevant. This requires careful selection of what to include and what to leave out. But this process should take place *after* you have assembled all your information, not while you are doing it.

Your style can also help you here. You can include more information in less space if you use clear, concise language and a brief style. But beware. Your report should also be easy to read; if you are too terse, people will find it difficult. It is a question of balance: you need to combine conciseness with an easy flow.

Seeing both sides

If you are presenting a report on a subject capable of more than one interpretation, or on which people can hold more than one opinion, you need to present both sides of the argument, and this means that you must be able to *see* both sides yourself. An objective report weighs up the various arguments and then makes recommendations or reaches conclusions based on the most convincing one. Show your readers that you have considered all the facts, that you have looked at the situation from all sides and that your conclusions are based on an objective assessment. If you do not, it will soon be apparent, and your report will lose its credibility.

Just as some people think they can influence their readers by only including facts that support their point of view, so there are some who believe that they can do the same thing by ignoring any interpretation of the facts except their own. Do not be tempted to try it. You may get away with it, but the chances are that you will not. One or more of your readers might realise that other interpretations are possible, and you could then find yourself faced with awkward questions for which you are not prepared.

Presenting your case

When you have considered the facts objectively, and reached your conclusion, that is the time to be persuasive. Argue logically, as we discussed in Chapter 2. Introduce facts from your analysis to back up your argument and present your own and other people's opinions if necessary. No one is going to object if you favour one solution or one side of the argument at this stage – in many cases they will expect you to do so. But do show that you have considered the facts objectively.

If you are presenting opinions, however, ensure that your readers are well aware that they *are* opinions. Do not mix facts with opinions. If you present something as a fact, then make sure you have the information to back it up. If it is an opinion, then say something like:

- This is believed to be the case.
- My opinion is ...
- In my opinion ...
- I believe that ...

Below is the 'Conclusion' section of a report; in it the writer argues persuasively and logically, and is quite clear about what is fact and what is opinion.

CONCLUSION

The above analysis leads me to the conclusion that handling our own sales and distribution is a perfectly feasible option. We have the space to do all our own storage. Of course the space we have is not a warehouse as such, but do we actually need a warehouse? The outhouse is dry, secure and spacious, and could very cheaply and easily be adapted to our needs. As I have said, all that is needed is shelving.

Our computer is quite capable of handling all our invoicing, and although we do not currently have the necessary software, that is something that can be readily purchased. The approximate cost of such a package is given in Appendix B, but since at this stage we are concerned only with the feasibility of the project, not the precise cost, I have not investigated the costs and advantages of the various packages.

We would obviously need to take on extra staff, and it has been said that this in itself would make the project unviable. However, it need not be so. I estimate that we would only need the equivalent of two extra in-house staff to handle the order processing, packing and invoicing. We could certainly afford that kind of increase in our staffing level. As for sales representatives, we need not employ our own. If we used freelance representatives, we would pay them on a commission basis, as suggested in Section 3. Although some people do not like employing freelance representatives on the grounds that they would not be fully committed to our products, my opinion is that they are likely to be more committed than our present distributors are. We would be a big fish in their little ponds, whereas to our present distributors, we are very small fry indeed.

In the light of all this, I believe that handling our own distribution is not only feasible, it is also desirable.

Dealing with opposing arguments

When you are discussing something at a meeting, other people can question you and argue against you, and you in turn can refute their arguments. When writing a report, you still need to deal with those arguments and questions as far as possible, but you do not have the opportunity to hear what they are. You therefore have to anticipate them and answer them in the course of your report.

If you have considered all sides of the argument when assessing your information, then you should not find it too hard to anticipate what the opposing arguments might be – you will probably have thought of most of them while doing your assessment. Since you will have considered these points before coming to your conclusion, you will also know what arguments you used when rejecting them.

But it is as well to think long and hard about this, and to make sure that there are no contrary arguments that you have not considered. The aim is to persuade your readers to accept your recommendation or conclusion, without having the issue clouded by an argument you could have refuted if you had thought of it. The example above shows how to anticipate and deal with such arguments. Notice that the writer does not specifically say, 'It could be argued that ... but my counter-argument is ...' The expressions used are:

- The space we have ... but ...
- Although we do not currently have the necessary software ...
- It has been said ... but ...
- Although some people do not like ...

EXERCISE 23

Look again at the report you did for Exercise 9. Now assume that, instead of simply providing information, you have been asked to recommend a change or changes to make your department or organisation better. Using the information you provided in your earlier report (and expanding on it if necessary), argue the case for the course of action you want to recommend.

Making Presentations

Presentations usually involve a range of different media, both verbal and visual. They require very careful planning, because the various elements must be fully integrated. A good presentation comes across as an almost seamless whole, not as a series of unconnected segments.

Most presentations involve a verbal element – the presenter will spend at least some time speaking about the subject. Other elements might include:

- **A video or DVD**. This is useful if you want to show a process or an activity. For example, a sales presentation might include a DVD showing how the product is made in order to get across the care that is taken. Or an outdoor pursuits centre might want to show the various activities they offer, and a video presentation is the best way to do that. However, when deciding whether to include a video or DVD, you need to take into account the fact that if the room needs to be darkened or the equipment must be rearranged in the middle of your presentation, it will disrupt your flow; you will have to weigh this disadvantage against the advantage of showing the process or activity.
- **A slide show**. This can take the form of a computerised show, overhead projection or photographic slides. Photographic slides can be used to show pictures that require no

movement for their impact (if movement is needed you should consider a video or DVD), such as a range of goods, holiday destinations, or the effects of different colour schemes. Other slides can be adapted for a wide range of purposes: for example to show charts, to summarise what you are saying, to pose questions for discussion or consideration, or to provide visual reinforcement of your oral presentation. And if they are computerised, you are able to introduce different kinds of animation to add interest.

- **A flipchart and pens or an interactive whiteboard**. These are usually used to illustrate points that arise as you are speaking, or in response to questions from the audience – in other words, when you want to make a point visually but do not have a slide prepared. If your slide show is not computerised, they can also be useful, for example, to show the development of a chart by adding lines, arrows, etc. (If you have a computerised slide show, then these devices can be incorporated into the animations you introduce.) If you have access to an interactive whiteboard (and know how to use it!) you will be able to incorporate more features than you can with a flipchart, but the latter is more common.

- **Product samples**. If you are making a presentation about a range of products, it might make for a more interesting event if you have samples on show with which you can demonstrate their features.

Of course you are unlikely to use all of these media in the same presentation, but you will probably use a combination of two or three.

Tips on Using Slides

- Use a variety of different formats – text, pictures, charts, etc. – so that your presentation does not become too monotonous.

- If you are using a computerised slide show and are able to animate your slides, it adds interest and enables you to develop a slide by adding elements to it as you speak.

- But you should not overdo the effects and animations; remember that your slides are there to illustrate your presentation or to provide additional information. If they are too complicated they will not do that and they will not be of any use, no matter how impressive they look.

- When showing text or graphics, ensure that your choice of colours does not make the slide difficult to decipher – there should be enough contrast for it to be easy to follow. And remember that something that looks good on your computer may not be so effective seen from the back of a large conference room.

- When using text, choose a font that is easy to read; for example, avoid calligraphic or 'script' fonts or those that do not conform to the standard letter shapes and formats.

- Ensure that text and graphics are large enough to be clear from all parts of the room.

- It is a good idea to provide paper copies of the slides as a handout for your audience – it saves them having to make too many notes while you are talking.

You should prepare your presentation carefully, so that you know what you are going to say and exactly how and when you intend to use your visual aids. You should make notes of what you want to say, including any particular words you need to remember. These notes can be as detailed as you think is necessary to ensure that you do not forget anything, but avoid writing out *exactly* what you want to say, word for word, as you may be tempted to read from your script instead of speaking naturally. There is no reason why you should not refer to your notes from time to time to ensure that you do not forget anything, or to remember a particularly useful expression, but it will be very boring for your audience if you read your whole presentation (unless you have an autocue and have had practice in using it).

Your talk must progress logically and smoothly, as explained in Chapter 2, but with the added complication that you need to plan for any visual effects you want to include. You should indicate in your notes when these are to be used – when to change a slide, when to pick up a particular product sample, when to switch on the video or DVD player – and how you are to introduce them so that they appear as a logical progression in the presentation, not an intrusion into it. It is a good idea to practise the whole presentation a few times before you actually have to appear before your audience, so that you have a fairly good idea of what you are going to say, how you are going to say it and how you intend to introduce the visual elements. This will help you to avoid too much hesitation and ensure that you do not have to refer to your notes too often.

When using text slides, remember that they are there either to provide a summary of what you are saying or to illustrate a particular point; in other words they are there to complement your delivery – and vice versa. You should never fall into the trap of reading your slides to the audience; it is unnecessary as they can read them for themselves, and it will only bore them. So, for example, if you are making a presentation on a building project, one slide might say:

This design is intended to provide:
- a carbon-neutral building
- a comfortable working environment
- room for expansion if necessary
- easy change of use in each element

You might show the whole slide and say, 'These are the essential principles behind this design. They were identified by the clients as their main priorities. We have aimed therefore to combine maximum flexibility with maximum sustainability and comfort.'

Alternatively, you might reveal each line individually and enlarge on that aspect, for example:

- 'It uses renewable energy sources, and there are facilities to ensure that all waste is recycled.'
- 'Because it is well insulated, it is also well sound-proofed, and every office has natural light. It is also intended that plants should form an integral part of the layout.'

In both these cases your words are complementing and expanding on what is on the slide. What you should *not* do is say, 'This design is intended to provide:

- a carbon-neutral building
- a comfortable working environment
- room for expansion if necessary
- easy change of use in each element.'

The audience can read that for themselves, and your words serve no useful purpose.

It is obviously important that you hold your audience's interest throughout the presentation, and if you read from a script or repeat what is on your slides their attention is bound to wander. But these are not the only pitfalls. You also need to vary the tone and pitch of your voice; *you* must be interested, enthusiastic even – a monotonous delivery will very quickly turn an audience off. In the same way, if you are showing slides you should try to show a variety of styles, so that people are not looking at the same format all the time. And as I have said, if the slide show is computerised, animation is useful in adding interest.

But even the best-delivered presentation can become tedious if it goes on for too long without a break. So if you are likely to be speaking for an hour or more, it is a good idea to break the session up with some kind of activity that involves the audience. Depending on the subject and the size and nature of the audience, such activities might involve a quiz of some kind, group discussions about an aspect of the presentation followed by feedback, or asking groups to examine and discuss product samples, even games. They should, of course, be relevant to the subject, and they should be integrated into the presentation in the same way as your visual aids. You should also be aware that a question-and-answer session, in which the audience ask you questions about what you have said so far, may well not work as such an activity because it depends on the audience taking the initiative; if they do not have any questions, then that part of the session will fall flat. So it is better for you to initiate the activity.

Shorter presentations probably will not need to be punctuated like this, but if you feel that an activity is relevant, there is no reason why you should not incorporate it.

CHAPTER 7
Common grammatical mistakes

If words are the building blocks of your communication, which you use to build sentences and paragraphs, then grammar is the mortar that holds them together. If you do not know how to use the words you choose, and the rules for putting them together, then you will end up with a jumble of unconnected words and phrases.

Some people cannot see the need for good grammar; they argue that as long as your audience can understand what you are saying, it does not have to be grammatically correct. When speaking it is true that you do not need to be too pedantic about grammar, but even then you must abide by certain basic rules. And when writing it is even more important, for two reasons. First, a document full of badly constructed sentences reflects badly on you – it is clumsy to read and it looks careless. Second, a badly constructed sentence may be understandable in one context, but in another the same poor construction could make the sentence vague or misleading. Look at these two sentences:

- We have a model with a 1.5 litre engine which has aluminium wheels.
- We have a model with a 1.5 litre engine which is guaranteed against corrosion.

Both sentences are incorrect, because the qualifying clauses 'which has aluminium wheels' and 'which is guaranteed ...' are not close enough to the noun they qualify, 'model'. However, with the first one, the reader at least knows what is meant, simply because an engine does not have wheels. The second one, which contains the same error, could be read in two ways – either the model is guaranteed against corrosion or the engine is. But which? So someone who is not concerned about grammar is likely to write or say things that are not only clumsy but also difficult to understand. And since clarity is one of the basic principles of business communication, you should not put yourself in a position where you have to explain what you mean.

In order to write or speak clearly, you do not need a detailed knowledge of grammar, but you should know the basic rules. This chapter will therefore not deal with the theoretical detail. What it will do is explain some of the basics and illustrate some of the errors most often found in business communications. It will also explain where you can occasionally break the rules to create a better flow or effect. But remember, there is a world of difference between knowing the rules and breaking them for effect and not knowing them and breaking them through ignorance.

Words are divided into different types, each with a particular role to play in building up a sentence. These divisions are known as parts of speech, and here we will look at each in turn.

Nouns and Pronouns

Nouns and pronouns are 'naming' words. They identify what it is we are talking about – for example, contract, client, him, she, Jennifer. As we saw in Chapter 4, every sentence must have a subject, and the subject will always be either a noun or a pronoun.

Every sentence must also have a predicate, which can either be just a verb ('He retired'), or a verb and an object ('He chaired the meeting'). The verb tells us what the subject did, and the object tells us what the subject did it to. This object will also always be a noun or a pronoun. So in the above example, 'he' is the subject, 'chaired' is the verb, and 'the meeting' is the object.

Nouns

Nouns are the words that actually name objects, places, people, ideas, etc. They are generally fairly easy to get right, but there are three main problems that can arise.

Nouns

There are five kinds of noun:

- common nouns, which name objects, like letter, desk, man

- abstract nouns, which name things you cannot see or touch, like strategy, export, idea

- proper nouns, which name specific people or places, like Peter, London, the Managing Director

- collective nouns, which name collections of people or things, like board, committee

- compound nouns, which consist of more than one word, like Peter Smith, John Brown & Co., Peters & Jones

---

- **Inappropriate use of capital letters**. Only proper nouns (those that name specific people or places) should begin with a capital letter. So you would say 'James Hunter', 'Birmingham', 'Thailand', 'Dorset County Council', 'the Sales Director', but you should *not* say 'the Balance Sheet', 'the Product', 'the Sales Figures'. Some people use capital letters for emphasis, but that is wrong – there are other ways of emphasising particular words, as we have seen.

  Some words can be either proper or common nouns, depending on the context. You might, for example, write about 'the Government' but 'a government'. In the first instance you are talking about a particular government, so the word is a title – a proper noun. In the second you are talking about any government, so it is a common noun.

- **Collective and compound nouns**. These are singular – they are one entity, even though they consist of several individuals. A committee of ten people is singular, because it is only one committee. Jones & Peterson is singular because, although Jones and Peterson are two people, they form one company. So all these collective or compound nouns should take singular verbs: 'The Board has decided to appoint a new director' not 'The Board *have* decided ...'; 'Jones & Peterson owes us money' not 'Jones & Peterson *owe* us money.' This rule is no longer as strictly applied as it was, however. Although you may still upset some people by using a plural verb with collective nouns such as 'board' or 'committee', it is now acceptable to do so with company names like 'Jones & Peterson'. So you could use either of the sentences shown on page 115. And just to confuse the issue, when you are talking about a board or a committee as individual people, you should use a plural verb. So you should say, 'The Committee have all been re-elected.'

Two common nouns connected by 'and' will normally be regarded as two nouns and therefore take a plural verb. But there are one or two expressions made up in this way that express one idea or concept, and which are therefore compound nouns. One example is 'bread and butter', as in 'The company's bread and butter is its retail trade.' In this context, 'bread and butter' is a single concept, not actual bread and butter.

- **Incorrect use of 'alternative'.** 'Alternative' means one of *two* choices. If there are three or more options open to you then you cannot have an alternative – the word to use then is 'choice' or 'option'. So you can say: 'There are two alternatives: we can either credit your account or replace the goods.' But you should say: 'There are *three* options: you can return the goods for full credit, we can replace them, or we can offer you an extra discount to compensate you.'

Pronouns

Pronouns are words that take the place of nouns. They are extremely useful little words; without them, our communications would be clumsy and difficult to follow. Consider the following passage: 'Jennifer Jameson has the draft contract. Peter Denton will ask Jennifer Jameson to give the draft contract to Sarah MacDonald so that Sarah MacDonald can check the draft contract to make sure that Jennifer Jameson has not overlooked any errors in the draft contract.' This is very long-winded and difficult. How much simpler it is when you use pronouns: 'Jennifer Jameson has the draft contract. *I* will ask *her* to give *it* to *you* so that *you* can make sure that *she* has not overlooked any errors in *it*.'

Pronouns

There are seven kinds of pronoun:

- personal pronouns, which relate to particular people or things, like 'I', 'her', 'it'

- possessive pronouns, which indicate possession, like 'his', 'her', 'my', 'our', 'your'

- reflexive pronouns, which are used when the object of the verb is the same as the subject: 'himself', 'myself', 'themselves', as in 'Peter gave himself a substantial pay rise.'

- demonstrative pronouns, which point something out, like 'this', 'that', 'those'

- relative pronouns, which introduce clauses that qualify a preceding noun or pronoun, like 'which' and 'that' in the above passage

- interrogative pronouns, which ask questions, like 'who?', 'what?', 'which?'

- indefinite pronouns, like 'anybody', 'somebody'

There are four common errors in the use of pronouns.

- **Ambiguous use**. You must ensure that your use of pronouns is not ambiguous. If it is, then either use the appropriate nouns instead or find another way of expressing yourself. A common ambiguity is this kind of thing: 'John Smith talked to James Jones about his letter.' Whose letter is it – John Smith's or James Jones's?
- **Incorrect use of the relative pronoun**. Because it takes the place of a noun, a pronoun can usually be the subject of a sentence. The only exception is the relative pronoun. Because relative pronouns introduce *clauses* not sentences (see under 'Phrases and Clauses' below), you cannot start a sentence with one. It is therefore wrong to say, 'Thank you for your order. Which is being processed today.' 'Which' should introduce a clause, which is part of a sentence, not the sentence itself. So the passage should read, 'Thank you for your order, which is being processed today.'
- **Confusion over the use of subjective and objective pronouns**. Some people have a problem with the different forms of the personal pronoun. There are two forms: subjective and objective. 'I', 'he', 'she', 'they' are subjective forms. As their name suggests, they are used when they are the subject of a sentence. 'Me', 'him', 'her', 'them' are objective forms, and are used when they are the object of a sentence. Most people can differentiate between them when using them on their own, but many get into difficulties when they use them in combination. For example, can you see what is wrong with these sentences?

  – Our Sales Manager and me will call on you tomorrow.
  – The Managing Director would like to see you and I at ten o'clock tomorrow.

  They both use the wrong form of the pronoun. In the first, the pronoun is part of the subject, so it should be in the subjective form. And in the second, the pronoun is part of the object, so it should be in the objective. The best way to ensure that you use the correct form is to use the pronoun on its own. So in the first sentence you would drop 'Our Sales Manager'. What would you say if you were calling on the client on your own? You would say, 'I will call ...' Similarly in the second sentence, if it were just you the Managing Director wanted to see, you would say, 'The Managing Director would like to see me ...' So you should use the same forms in combination with the accompanying nouns.
- **The pronoun 'none'**. This is a word that causes some difficulty. It is short for 'not one', and is therefore singular. So you should say, 'None of the Committee's decisions was acceptable to the Board', not 'None of the Committee's decisions *were* acceptable ...' It is now quite common to see 'none' used with a plural verb, but there are still some people who object to this usage, and it is therefore better to use the correct form.

Verbs

Verbs are 'doing' or 'being' words. They tell us what the subject of a sentence does or did, is or was. As we saw in Chapter 4, every sentence must have a verb. There are two common problems involving verbs.

- **Splitting the infinitive**. The infinitive is the 'to' form of the verb: 'to write', 'to meet', 'to complain'. The rules of grammar say that you should not split an infinitive – in other words, nothing should come between 'to' and the rest of the verb. You should therefore not say, 'We need to clearly identify our key markets.' In trying to avoid splitting the infinitive, there are three places you can put the word that is splitting it: before the infinitive, after the infinitive and at the end of the sentence. When you are faced with a split infinitive, try all three to see which sounds best:

- We need clearly to identify our key markets.
- We need to identify clearly our key markets.
- We need to identify our key markets clearly.

In this case the third version sounds better, but there will be other sentences in which one of the other positions would be better.

However, you should not be too dogmatic. Split infinitives are becoming more common, and although you will find that in most cases your sentences will read more smoothly if you avoid them, there will be times, especially in longer sentences, when it will actually sound *less* clumsy if you split an infinitive. Take for example, the following sentence: 'We appear to deliberately avoid making our clients comfortable while they are waiting to see a partner.' If you try the three 'non-split' versions you will probably conclude that, although putting 'deliberately' before the infinitive may be the best of the three options, the sentence actually reads better as it is.

- **Using a singular verb with a plural subject and vice versa.** As we have seen, the verb and its subject must agree in number, so a singular subject must take a singular verb, and a plural subject a plural verb. This may seem obvious, and few people would make the mistake of saying something like 'I were in a meeting' or 'Peter and Janet was asked to make a presentation.' However, there are pitfalls. First, the adjectives 'each' and 'every' have the effect of making nouns singular. So although you would say, 'All directors are entitled to a share option' you would say, '*Every* director *is* entitled to a share option.' The same applies when the subject is two nouns: 'All directors and managers are entitled ...', but '*Every* director and manager *is* entitled ...' So even though you would expect the subject to be plural because it consists of two nouns, the word 'every' makes it singular.

Another problem is caused by clauses and phrases that are in parenthesis (written almost as an aside). Although you would write 'The desk and the computer are to be moved to the new office', since there are two nouns and the subject is therefore plural, you should write 'The desk, together with the computer, *is* to be moved ...' Here, because the reference to the computer is enclosed by commas, it means that it is an aside, almost an afterthought. The subject is actually just the desk, so the verb is singular.

A similar problem arises when the subject and the verb are separated. It can then be difficult to see what the subject actually is. Look at these two sentences:

- The aim of the consultant's thoroughly researched and clearly explained proposals are to make the company more productive.
- My expenses, including subsistence allowance, is attached.

In the first sentence, the subject is 'aim' not 'proposals', so the verb should be singular. The confusion arises because the noun nearest to the verb is 'proposals'. And in the second, the subject is 'expenses', not 'allowance', so the verb should be plural. If you are in doubt, you can check what the subject is by saying 'what?' before the predicate. So in the second sentence, the answer to the question 'What is attached?' is 'my expenses', which is plural.

Adjectives and Adverbs

Adjectives and adverbs are 'qualifying' words. They add to and extend the meaning of other words. As we saw in Chapter 5, one of the main stylistic errors people make is to use vague or meaningless qualifiers – 'nice', 'really', 'quite'. But used correctly, adjectives and adverbs can help you express yourself more precisely and add considerably to your audience's understanding of what you are saying. Of course, as we have seen, used badly, they will just make it harder to understand.

Adjectives

Adjectives qualify (describe) nouns: 'a substantial profit', 'the correct spelling', 'an easy decision'. Some forms of verbs can also be used as adjectives, as in 'a written contract', or 'the driving force'. Adjectives can also compare things, as in 'the best way forward' or 'This company offers a better service than that one.' The '-er' form is called the comparative and the '-est' form the superlative.

There are four problems to beware of when using adjectives.

- **Incorrect use of the superlative**. The comparative form of an adjective is used to compare two things; the superlative is used for three or more. This is an easy rule to follow when you are making a direct comparison, as in 'Norma's idea is better than Ken's.' It sounds quite wrong to say 'Norma's idea is best than Ken's' and few people would make that mistake. But what about 'Of the two plans, Norma's is the best'? That does not sound quite so wrong, but you are still comparing two things, so you should in fact use the comparative form: 'Of the two plans, Norma's is better.' You should only use 'best' if there are three or more plans. This rule is less strictly adhered to than it used to be, but you might still cause a few raised eyebrows if you ignore it.

- **Omitting an article**. The words 'the', 'a' and 'an' qualify nouns, so they are adjectives, although they are usually called articles. 'The' is the definite article (it means you are talking about something specific and definite), and 'a' and 'an' are indefinite articles (they mean you are talking about something indefinite). When you are talking about two people or things, there can be a tendency to leave out the second article, as in 'I enclose copies of the letter and order' or 'I enclose a catalogue and order form'. If in each of these cases there are two documents, then the construction is grammatically incorrect – there should be an article before the second noun: 'I enclose copies of the letter and the order' and 'I enclose a catalogue and an order form.' Only if the two nouns form a single item should you leave out the second article: 'the Chairman and Managing Director', for example, means that one person fills both those roles.

  There is no real problem with this if it is clear that there are two things, as in the first example – the word 'copies' indicates that there are two documents. But what about the second? Is the order form part of the catalogue or separate? As it stands, the sentence says that it is part of the catalogue. If there are two documents, then the writer *must* include the second article for clarity. This is an example of how a construction that is understandable in one context can be confusing in another.

- **Incorrect use of 'either'**. 'Either' as an adjective refers to one of only *two* things. You can therefore write: 'This carpet comes in beige or green. Either colour would suit the decor you have in mind.' But if there are more than two colours you should not use 'either'. Instead you should say: 'This carpet comes in beige, green or gold. Any one of these colours would suit the decor you have in mind.'

- **Confusing 'less' and 'fewer'.** 'Less' is used for quantity, and 'fewer' for number. So you can have 'less work', 'less confusion', 'less chance of promotion', because you are talking about a quantity of work, confusion or chance. But if the noun is in the plural, then you must use 'fewer' because you are talking about the numbers involved, so you would say 'fewer employees', 'fewer problems', 'fewer chances of success'.

Adverbs

As their name implies, adverbs qualify verbs – they tell you how, when and where the action of the sentence took place. So in the sentence 'I went there yesterday', 'there' and 'yesterday' are adverbs, telling the audience where and when you went. But they do not *only* qualify verbs. They can qualify other parts of speech as well: in 'very difficult', 'very' qualifies an adjective; in 'just after' 'just' qualifies a preposition; in 'superbly well', 'superbly' qualifies another adverb.

Like adjectives, some adverbs can have comparative and superlative forms. When the adverb consists of one syllable, like 'soon', it forms the comparative and superlative like an adjective: 'sooner', 'soonest'. When it is a long word, and particularly when it ends in '-ly', the comparative and superlative are formed by using 'more' and 'most' before the adverb. So the comparative of 'clearly' is 'more clearly' and the superlative is 'most clearly'. Of course, not all adverbs have comparative and superlative forms; you cannot, for example, say 'more very difficult' or 'most just after'.

The main grammatical problems associated with the use of adverbs are:

- **Confusing positioning.** Make sure that the position of your adverb does not cause confusion, especially when using 'only'. Look at the following sentence: 'I only asked you last week to submit your expenses on the approved form.' As this stands, it means that I only *asked* you, I did not order you. If I had meant that it was only last week that I asked you, I should have said, 'I asked you only last week ...' The rule therefore is that the adverb should go as close as possible to the word it qualifies. But you do not need to be too dogmatic, as long as there is no doubt about the meaning, and as long as the sentence does not sound clumsy.

- **Using double adverbs.** When you are using a double adverb, as in 'not only ... but also', you must keep the parts of the sentence which follow them 'in parallel'. This means that they must both have the same construction. So you should not say: 'You have not only failed to supply our order, but also to give a reason for non-delivery'. 'Not only' is followed by the past participle 'failed', while 'but also' is followed by the infinitive 'to give'. For the sentence to be in parallel, they should either *both* be followed by the past participle or *both* by the infinitive. (You do not have to worry too much about the terms 'past participle' and 'infinitive'; the principle is that you must use the same form of the verb in both parts of the sentence, either the '-ed' form or the 'to' form.) So you can write either:

  – You have not only failed to supply our order, but also omitted to give a reason for the non-delivery.

  or

  – You have failed not only to supply our order but also to give a reason for the non-delivery.

- **Using 'hardly' and 'scarcely'**. There is a similar problem of keeping elements of a sentence in parallel with the use of the adverbs 'hardly' and 'scarcely'. Can you see what is wrong with the following sentence? 'I had hardly put the phone down than your parcel arrived.' This is a fairly common construction, but it is wrong. 'Hardly' is an adverb expressing time, and 'than' is a conjunction expressing comparison. So the two do not go together. If you are using an adverb expressing time in this construction, then the conjunction should also express time: 'I had hardly put the phone down *when* your parcel arrived.' Although it is quite common to see 'hardly' and 'scarcely' used with 'than', it is incorrect and sounds clumsy, so you should always use 'when' with them.

Prepositions

A preposition is a word that shows the relationship of one thing or person to another. So in the sentence 'The meeting will be in the boardroom', 'in' is a preposition which shows the relationship between the meeting and the boardroom. 'By', 'to', 'on', 'from' and 'with' are also examples of prepositions. A preposition should always be followed by a noun or a pronoun (since it is showing a relationship to a person or a thing). When it is followed by a pronoun it should take the objective form: 'to me', 'from him', 'about her'.

There are three things you need to be careful of when using prepositions.

- **Ending a sentence with a preposition**. The strict rule is that you should not end a sentence with a preposition. So instead of 'Mrs Graham is the person I spoke to you about', you should say 'Mrs Graham is the person about whom I spoke to you.' However, when speaking you do not need to worry too much about this rule. And even when writing, it need not be applied too strictly – indeed there will be occasions when trying to avoid ending with a preposition will make your sentence so clumsy it becomes absurd, as in the quote attributed to Sir Winston Churchill: 'This is something up with which I will not put.'
- **Using the wrong preposition**. Certain verbs and adjectives are associated with particular prepositions, and you must use the correct form. Below is a list of those that are most often used incorrectly, with the correct ones in brackets.
  - accompanied with (by)
  - different to or than (from)
  - oblivious to (of)
  - opposite from (to)
  - prevail on (upon)
  - replace with (by)

  There are also some words which can take two or more prepositions, depending on the meaning. So if you use them with the wrong preposition you will not just give a poor impression, you will actually change the meaning of your sentence. Here are the most commonly confused ones.
  - agree to (a proposal)
    agree with (a person)
  - concerned at (something that has happened)
    concerned for (a person)
  - correspond with (means 'write to')
    correspond to (means 'be the same as')

- differ from (means 'be different from')
  differ with (means 'disagree with')
- entrust (something) to (a person)
  entrust (someone) with (a thing)
- impatient with (a person)
  impatient of (authority, criticism, etc.)
- interfere in (a dispute, etc.)
  interfere with (a person)

- **Incorrect use of 'among'**. 'Among' applies only when you are writing about three or more people or things. If there are only two, then you must use 'between'. So you might say 'You can divide the territory among the four of you', but you should say 'You can divide the territory *between* the two of you.'

Conjunctions

Conjunctions are 'connecting' words. They are used to join two or more words, phrases or clauses together. So in the phrase 'you and me', 'and' is a conjunction. There are two kinds of conjunction:

- **co-ordinating** conjunctions, like 'and', 'but', 'nor', 'or', which combine words, phrases or clauses of equal weight

- **subordinating** conjunctions, like 'because', 'before', 'since', 'although', 'unless', which connect a subordinate clause to the main one

---

Subordinating Conjunctions and Subordinate Clauses

Unlike co-ordinating conjunctions, subordinating conjunctions only connect clauses, not words or phrases. And the clauses they introduce are called subordinate clauses. This means that they are subordinate to the main clause – the main part of the sentence; they depend on the main clause for their relevance. In the sentence, 'I will take no further action unless I hear from you', 'I hear from you' could not stand as a sentence on its own – it only has meaning in this context as part of the whole sentence. In the sentence 'I have searched our records, but I am afraid that I cannot find your order', 'I am afraid that I cannot find your order' is not dependent on the first clause – it could form a sentence on its own and still make sense. That is why it is introduced by the co-ordinating conjunction 'but'.

It used to be considered incorrect to start a sentence with a conjunction, but the practice has become so common that it is now quite acceptable. There are, however, still five potential problems with conjunctions.

- **The double conjunctions 'either ... or' and 'neither ... nor'**. We saw under 'Adverbs' on page 120 how the two sections of a sentence introduced by a double adverb like 'not only ...but also' must be in parallel. The same applies to double conjunctions. So you should not say, 'The situation is that you either take remedial action or we shall take our business elsewhere.' 'Either' comes after the subject of the first clause, but 'or' comes *before* the subject of the second. They should both be before the subjects. So the sentence should read 'The situation is that either you take remedial action or we take our business elsewhere.'

Another problem some people have with these double conjunctions is that they use a plural verb with them, even when the nouns are singular. For example, they might say 'Neither invoice 23765 nor invoice 24534 have been paid.' What this means is that invoice 23765 has not been paid, nor has invoice 24534 been paid. You are simply replacing two verbs with one, so it should remain a singular verb: 'Neither invoice 23765 nor invoice 24534 *has* been paid.' Of course, if the nouns are plural, then you *should* use the plural verb: 'Neither the sales representatives nor the demonstrators *are* happy with their pay increases.'

- **Choosing the right type of conjunction to link clauses**. When joining two clauses, you should think carefully. If you use a co-ordinating conjunction to introduce a subsidiary clause, you will give the clause too much weight. There is a subtle difference between these two sentences:
  - The Managing Director will be at our sales conference this week, and he will not be able to give you a reply until next Monday.
  - The Managing Director will be at our sales conference this week, and therefore he will not be able to give you a reply until next Monday.

  In the first sentence, the two clauses are equal. This means that although the two ideas are connected, the connection is not particularly close. The fact that the Managing Director cannot give you a reply may be only partly due to his being at the sales conference; the implication is that there are other factors as well. In the second sentence, the second clause is very definitely tied to the first by the word 'therefore'. He cannot give you a reply *because* he will be at the sales conference. You should therefore choose your conjunctions with care, and not use a co-ordinating one in a subordinating role.

- **Using conjunctions to link unrelated ideas**. Conjunctions should only be used to connect clauses that deal with related ideas. You should therefore not say something like: 'We had to make two people redundant this month and sales were up by 25 per cent.' It sounds as though the two events were connected. As we saw in Chapter 4, each sentence should contain a single idea or two related ideas. If the ideas are not related, they should be in separate sentences.

- **Confusing 'as' and 'like'**. When expressing a similarity, you can use the conjunction 'as' or the preposition 'like', as in 'We should be dealing with complaints as they do' or 'We need a computer system like theirs.' But the two words are not interchangeable. Like all prepositions, 'like' can only be used with a noun or a pronoun. If the word is to introduce a clause, you should use the conjunction 'as'. So it is wrong to say: 'Why can we not achieve a consistently high quality, like they do'? You should say '*as* they do', because 'they do' is a clause, not a noun.

- **Separating a subordinate clause from the main clause**. If, in checking your work, you find a sentence that starts with a subordinating conjunction, you should look at it very carefully because, as we have seen, a subordinating conjunction introduces a subordinate clause – one that depends on the main clause for its meaning – and it cannot be a sentence on its own. So you cannot say: 'I am afraid we will not be renewing our contract with you. Because, despite several warnings, you have not provided the level of service we require.' The second part of the passage does not make sense on its own because it is only there to qualify the first part. You must therefore write it as one sentence: 'I am afraid we will not be renewing our contract with you because, despite several warnings, you have not provided the level of service we require.'

However, if the passage really is a complete sentence, just with the subordinate clause before rather than after the main one, then there is no reason why you cannot start it with the subordinating conjunction. The above sentence could, therefore, be written: 'Because, despite several warnings, you have not provided the level of service we require, I am afraid we will not be renewing our contract with you.' This changes the emphasis slightly, from the fact that you will not be renewing the contract to the fact that your correspondent has not provided the level of service you require, and is quite acceptable. But you do need to ensure that both the subordinate and the main clause are there in the one sentence.

Phrases and Clauses

Phrases and clauses are groups of words within a sentence. We have already seen some of the uses of clauses in the discussion of conjunctions above. The difference between them and phrases is that they have a subject and a predicate and phrases do not. For most practical purposes, however, this difference is of purely academic interest.

There are many different kinds of phrase and clause, but they are really of interest only to grammarians. The main ones we need to be aware of in day-to-day business communication are adjectival and adverbial phrases and clauses – the ones that act as adjectives or adverbs, qualifying other words. The following sentences contain examples:

- Thank you for your cheque, which arrived today.
- After two weeks without a response, I decided to call on the customer.

In the first sentence, 'which arrived today' is an adjectival clause: it describes the cheque. In the second, 'after two weeks without a response' is an adverbial phrase: it describes when I decided, just as an adverb would.

There are just three problems to beware of with phrases and clauses.

- **Separating adjectival and adverbial clauses and phrases from the words they qualify**. This is perhaps the most common. Look at the following sentences:
  - No one may remove anything from the stationery cupboard except the Manager's PA.
  - We have had to ask you to deliver the new machine four times.

  In the first sentence, it sounds as though the only thing you can remove from the stationery cupboard is the Manager's PA! The adjectival phrase 'except the Manager's PA' should go next to the pronoun it qualifies, 'no one'. In the second, it sounds as though we wanted you to deliver the machine four times, because the adverbial phrase 'four times' is closer to the verb 'deliver' than the one it qualifies, 'ask'. So these sentences should read:
  - No one except the Manager's PA may remove anything from the stationery cupboard.
  - We have had to ask you four times to deliver the new machine.

  Now the adjectival and adverbial phrases are close to the words they qualify, and your meaning is clear.

- **Leaving hanging participles**. The following sentence contains an example of this error: 'Arriving at the conference centre, the Manager had left.' The adjectival phrase 'arriving at the conference centre' has nothing to qualify, and the present participle 'arriving' which introduces it is therefore left hanging – hence the term 'hanging participle'. It looks as though it qualifies 'the Manager', but that makes the sentence nonsensical. It needs to be rewritten so that the phrase has something to qualify. So you should say: 'Arriving at the conference sentence, *we found that* the Manager had left.' Now the phrase qualifies the pronoun 'we' and the sentence makes sense.

- **Omitting the second subject**. When two clauses are joined by a conjunction, it is quite common to leave out the subject of the second clause if it is the same as the subject of the first. So you can say: 'I hope this clarifies the situation and look forward to hearing from you' instead of '... and *I* look forward ...' But some people make the mistake of leaving out the second subject when it is different from the first. They might say: 'Your queries are being investigated and will be in touch shortly.' This sounds as though 'your queries' will be in touch shortly, which is, of course, absurd. The reason for the confusion is that the subject of the second clause is not the same as the subject of the first. The person who will be in touch is the writer, so it should be: 'Your queries are being investigated and I will be in touch shortly.'

EXERCISE 24

Correct the grammar of the following passages.

1. The Board was asked to carefully consider the Proposal. It was only given conditional approval after a lengthy discussion.

2. On Wednesday, Keith Hamilton had a meeting with Simon Kitson. He said that the following week he would be in Paris, where the company have their European office, so he could discuss the contract then.

3. We have had a good response to our advertisement for a Sales Manager, and Emma Johnson would like to discuss the applications with you and I on Tuesday.

4. I do not mind you asking for time off, but it would be nice to occasionally see you working late as well. You appear to be getting rather behind with your work. Which is affecting the efficiency of the whole department.

5. You say that you have not seen the delivery note and invoice. Your accountant and me have had a long discussion about this, and I think you will find that he has copies.

6. The Committee have decided that every member, together with his or her partner, have the right to use the facilities of the centre.

7. Having considered all the estimates, I believe either we should accept Axis's or Mainland Distribution's. None of the other firms were able to match their prices or delivery times.

8. Please can you see to it that every secretary and clerk, including the directors' PAs, are made aware of the new house style. We must not only ensure that we create a good image but also a consistent one.

9. We can offer a choice of three conference rooms, either of which would suit your requirements, and we will serve lunch at 12.30 p.m. as requested.

10. I am afraid that I differ from you over the best way forward for the development. Looking at the two plans, the layout of the second is much more flexible.

CHAPTER 8
Punctuation

Punctuation is a form of signalling, showing how you intend your document to be read in order to make its meaning quite clear. When you speak, you 'punctuate' your speech automatically: your voice rises at the end of a question, you pause at appropriate moments, or you might use forms of words such as 'by the way', or 'that means'. When you are writing, punctuation takes the place of these aural signals.

You need to think carefully about how you punctuate your documents, because it does not happen naturally, as it does in speech. Most punctuation marks indicate pauses, and different marks indicate different lengths of pause: generally, the pause for a full stop is longer than that for a semicolon, while a comma has the shortest pause of all.

You need to strike a balance between too many and too few punctuation marks. If you have too many, your document is broken up too much and becomes disjointed. If you use too few it becomes difficult to follow. The following passage has no punctuation marks at all. As you can see, it is very difficult to see what the writer means.

```
I am afraid that owing to the fact that the Managing Director is out of the
office at the moment it is not possible to agree to your request immediately not
that it is likely to be turned down of course but we do need his approval for
agreements of this nature however he will be back next week and I will make sure
that he deals with it as soon as possible.
```

Here is the same passage, but over-punctuated.

```
I am afraid that, owing to the fact, that the Managing Director is out of the
office, at the moment, it is not possible to agree to your request, immediately.
Not that it is likely to be turned down, of course; but we do need his approval
for agreements of this nature. However, he will be back next week; and I will
make sure that he deals with it, as soon as possible.
```

As you can see, it is very disjointed to read – almost jerky, in fact. Now let us see how it looks when properly punctuated.

```
I am afraid that, owing to the fact that the Managing Director is out of the
office at the moment, it is not possible to agree to your request immediately –
not that it is likely to be turned down of course, but we do need his approval
for agreements of this nature. However, he will be back next week and I will make
sure that he deals with it as soon as possible.
```

This version is easier to read, and the sense is quite clear the first time you read it.

Punctuation is to a certain extent a matter of style, but there are certain rules that must be followed if your documents are to make sense to your readers. In this chapter we will be looking at both the rules and the points of style governing punctuation marks.

The Purposes of Punctuation

Punctuation serves four main purposes.

- **It divides passages up**. Punctuation separates what you are writing into easily absorbed parts: sentences, clauses and phrases. Look at the following sentence: 'I am enclosing our latest catalogue, in which you will find all our current models.' The comma breaks the sentence into two parts, which are easier to read than one long one.

- **It indicates a relationship**. It can signal the relationship between one part of a sentence and another, as in the following: 'The catalogue (which has just been published) contains details of our current models.' The brackets indicate that the clause they enclose is an aside, not part of the main theme of the sentence.

- **It differentiates between two meanings**. An example of this is in the following two sentences:
  - Sales are up by 15% more than we budgeted for.
  - Sales are up by 15%, more than we budgeted for.

  Although exactly the same words are used, the two sentences have different meanings; the difference is in the comma.

- **It creates emphasis**. You can emphasise certain words or phrases, as in 'There is only one possible outcome in this situation – bankruptcy.' Using the dash in this way emphasises the word 'bankruptcy'.

Full Stops

The rules for using full stops are quite simple and widely understood. There are just two occasions when they are used.

- to end a sentence, as in 'Mr Graham has passed your letter to me.'
- after initials or abbreviations, as in 'P.J. Darwin', 'Inc.', 'Co.' But note that a full stop is not necessary after a contraction – an abbreviation in which the first and last letters are the same as in the full word, like 'Dr' ,'Mr', 'Ltd' – or between the letters in abbreviations such as 'BBC' or 'USA'. Then it is a matter of your own personal choice.

Commas

The rules governing commas are not as straightforward, or as definite, as those for other punctuation marks. They are the most flexible, and where you use them is largely a matter of taste. They can be used in a variety of situations.

Separating words or phrases in a list

When you are listing items, they should be separated by commas, as in 'We can offer a choice of beige, black, dark blue or grey trim.' Note that it is not usual to have a comma before the final 'and' or 'or' – only put them in if it is necessary for clarity. If the list is a complex one, where each item is a long phrase or a clause, it might be better to use a semicolon (see under 'Semicolons' below).

You can also use commas to separate adjectives qualifying the same noun, as in 'Please enclose a large, self-addressed envelope.' In this context it is a matter of preference; as long as the passage is easy to follow, it is not essential to use commas. One situation when you *must* leave it out is when the adjective and the noun actually go together to form a compound noun. In 'Please supply a large filing cabinet', for example, 'filing' does not qualify the noun, it is part of it. A filing cabinet is very different from an ordinary cabinet, so filing does not describe the cabinet in the way that 'large' does. So you should not have a comma between 'large' and 'filing'.

Joining two clauses

When two clauses are joined by a co-ordinating conjunction, you can use a comma or not. So you can write either:

• I strongly disagree and I think you should reconsider.

or

• I strongly disagree, and I think you should reconsider.

Whether you use a comma in this context will depend not only on your own preference, but also on the length of the sentence and the amount of separation you want to indicate. If your sentence is long, you may want to put in a comma, introducing a pause so that the reader can absorb what he or she has read so far. If the ideas in the clauses are not closely related, you might put in a comma to increase the impression of separation, whereas if they are very closely linked you might leave it out so as to bring them closer in the reader's mind.

Separating an introductory signal

When you use a signalling device to indicate the direction your document is about to take, you can use a comma to separate it from the rest of the sentence, as in 'Finally, may I offer my congratulations on your success this year.' This is again a matter of personal preference, but generally that slight degree of separation makes the sentence easier to follow.

Creating parenthesis

You can use commas as parentheses, when you insert something which either expands on the main part of the sentence without affecting it, or qualifies part of it. Here are two examples:

• This is not, I am sure, what the Board had in mind.
• Mr Jones, the Senior Partner, will be in touch shortly.

In both these cases, the main part of the sentence stands perfectly well on its own, without the section in parenthesis.

If something is in parenthesis, you should always signal that with some punctuation device, otherwise your reader will not know how it fits in with the sentence as a whole. But you can also use brackets and dashes for this, as indicated below.

Introducing quotations

You must use either a comma or a colon to introduce direct speech or a quotation of a full sentence from another source. You are unlikely to use direct speech very much in business writing, but you might find yourself quoting from another source. If so, you should say: 'Jonathan Wallace's report says, "We must encourage our employees to participate fully in the decisions that govern their working lives."'

If you are only quoting a few words, then you should not introduce the quotation with a comma. So you would say: 'Jonathan Wallace's report says that we should encourage our employees to participate fully in "the decisions that govern their working lives".' In this case, only the last part of the clause is a direct quotation, so no comma is used to introduce it.

Separating phrases and clauses for easier reading

Depending on the length and complexity of a sentence, you can use commas to separate some of the constituent phrases and clauses to make it easier to read:

- Since you have not replied to my letter, I assume that you agree with my suggestion.
- Reading your report, I was struck by its clarity.

In neither of these sentences are the commas essential, but they do help to make them easier to follow.

Avoiding confusion

Commas can be used to avoid confusion, even in situations where you would not normally use them. Look at the following sentence: 'The outfits are available in red and white and brown and beige.' One might guess from the way it is expressed that they are available in two combinations of two colours, not in four individual colours. But to make your meaning absolutely clear, it would be better to say, 'The outfits are available in red and white, and brown and beige.'

As this section shows, the use of commas is largely a matter of taste and style, but you should not overuse them, otherwise you will introduce too many pauses and your document will become disjointed. Look at the following sentence: 'However, if we invest in new plant, and the market falls again, as it could easily do, we might, conceivably, find ourselves with too much production capacity, which could, perhaps, cause even graver problems.' None of these commas is actually wrong, but there are just too many of them. We are forced to read the sentence in jerks. You need to use your discretion and cut out a few inessential ones so that the sentence flows.

Semicolons

The semicolon is probably the most undervalued of all punctuation marks; it can be extremely useful, yet it is very seldom used. Like the comma, its use is to a certain extent a matter of personal preference and style. Basically, it is used to indicate a longer pause than a comma would give, but shorter than a full stop. There are four situations in which it is useful.

Making a clear separation

A semicolon can be used to separate statements that are closely connected, but not so closely as to justify either a comma or a conjunction, as in 'I like your proposal; it is well thought out and workable.' Here the two ideas are connected, so it would look wrong if they were two separate sentences. On the other hand, 'I like your proposal because it is well thought out and workable' ties the two ideas too closely together. It sounds as though you like the proposal *only* because it is well thought out and workable.

Emphasising a statement

A semicolon can be used to emphasise a statement or make it more punchy. As you can see if you read the above example again, almost any statement after a semicolon is given extra emphasis. Here is another example: 'We must improve our productivity; we face bankruptcy if we do not.' The second part of the sentence stands out starkly – far more so than if it had been written 'We must improve our productivity because we face bankruptcy if we do not.' But note that this device can only be used to emphasise a whole clause; single words or phrases should be emphasised by using a dash (see below).

Conveying contrast

Semicolons can be used to balance contrasting statements, as in: 'We offer a home delivery service; other firms do not.' As in the above examples, the emphasis is on the second statement, but the main purpose of the semicolon here is to highlight the contrast between your service and that of other firms.

Separating longer items in a list

As we saw under 'Commas' above, items in a list are usually separated by commas. When the items are longer, however, semicolons might be better. There are no hard and fast rules about this, but a good rule of thumb is that semicolons should be used when the items themselves contain commas, or when they are clauses. Look at the following examples:

- I recommend the following: that we increase our sales staff by five; that we double our advertising budget; and that we introduce more stringent quality control measures.
- We have three main requirements: high-quality, durable materials; reasonable prices; and fast, reliable delivery.

In the first sentence, the items in the list are clauses. To separate them only with commas would make them appear to run into each other. In the second, there are commas in two of the items in the list. If the items themselves were separated by commas, it would be confusing to read.

Note that, unlike commas, when you are using semicolons in this way, you *should* have a semicolon before the final 'and' or 'or'.

Colons

Colons have only three uses:

- They are used to introduce lists, especially those where the items are separated by semicolons (they are not essential if the items are short and are separated by commas), as in: 'I would be grateful if you could let me have your cheque in payment of the following invoices which are overdue: No. 14352 of 6 January, No. 21345 of 29 January and No. 25431 of 10 February.'
- They can be used to indicate two sides of the same theme; the first part of the sentence makes a statement, and the second part explains it. Here are two examples:
  - The solution is simple: train more operators.
  - The reasons are the same in both cases: we are undervaluing our key staff.
- They can be used instead of commas to introduce direct speech or quotations.

Brackets

There are two kinds of brackets:

- round brackets (also called parentheses), which are the kind we are most familiar with: ().
- square brackets, which look like this: [].

They serve different purposes, and should therefore not be confused.

Round brackets

Using round brackets in most contexts is a bit like saying, 'By the way' in speech. They are used for asides, for indicating that a passage is not part of the main theme of the sentence, but is added by way of explanation or comment. So you might write: 'There is still £2,470 outstanding on your account (see enclosed statement).' The part in brackets is an extension of the sentence, but it does not express part of its theme or idea.

Commas, Brackets or Dashes?

If you want to put a passage in parenthesis you have three options: you can enclose it in commas, round brackets or dashes. But which should you use? The rule of thumb is that commas denote less of a pause than brackets, which denote less of a pause than dashes. So you can choose your punctuation marks according to the degree of separation you want: commas will connect the passage closely to the rest of the sentence and brackets less closely, while dashes will separate it out most of all. You can see this in the following examples:

- Jackie Milton, the new Chief Executive, will be visiting your department tomorrow.
- Jackie Milton (the new Chief Executive) will be visiting your department tomorrow.
- Jackie Milton – the new Chief Executive – will be visiting your department tomorrow.

In the first sentence, the passage in commas is a simple description of Jackie Milton, and is closely linked to the first part of the sentence. In the second, the writer is saying the equivalent of 'and by the way she is the new Chief Executive'; the assumption is that the reader may not already know that. And in the third, the writer appears to want to emphasise the fact that she is the new Chief Executive, and therefore separates the passage from the main clause even more, making it stand out.

Beware of using brackets for very long passages. They break up the sentence and cause the reader to pause, and if the break is too long the reader will lose track of what the sentence is about. Consider the following passage: 'Susan King (who was appointed Managing Director to succeed Martin Wilson, who resigned in January) will be addressing the conference next week.' The passage in brackets is so long that by the time it ends, the reader may have difficulty remembering what the subject of the sentence is. Anything that long should be placed between commas, as in: 'Susan King, who was appointed Managing Director to succeed Martin Wilson, who resigned in January, will be addressing the conference next week.' Now the break in the sentence is not quite so long, and it flows more smoothly.

Round brackets are also used to enclose explanations of terms or abbreviations, or to show reference sources. It is normal practice to explain an abbreviation or technical term only once, the first time you use it. So you might write: 'A great deal of the development work in this area is done by NGOs (non-governmental organisations). Unfortunately, these NGOs do not always co-ordinate their efforts to best effect.'

As we have seen, if you are writing a report and referring to, or quoting from, someone else's work, you should acknowledge their contribution. This is often done by putting your source in brackets after you have referred to it: 'A leading human resources management expert believes that all managerial personnel should be retrained in the techniques of managing change (H.K. Burton, *Human Resources Management in a Changing Environment*).' If you have an acknowledgements section in your report, and the full title of the source you are referring to is shown there, then you might just show the author (and possibly the page on which the reference appears).

Square brackets

You will not often need to use square brackets, but it is as well to know how their use differs from that of round ones.

Square brackets are used when you are quoting directly from another source and you want to add something of your own – usually an expansion or explanation. The following passage shows an example: 'Bani Desai's report states: "If we wish to improve our image then we must ensure that our treatment of them [the customers] is not only courteous but also helpful and efficient."' This indicates that *you* have inserted 'the customers' to explain who 'them' refers to.

Dashes

However and wherever you use them, dashes increase the emphasis of what you are saying. The part of the sentence after the dash – or between the dashes in the case of two – will always carry more emphasis than without the dash. They have four main functions.

- As we have seen, two dashes can be used to put something in parenthesis, when you want more emphasis and greater separation of the passage from the rest of the sentence than brackets provide.
- Two dashes can also be used to pull together or summarise several items, as in: 'Computers, filing cabinets, printers, bookshelves – in fact all office equipment – should be listed.'

- One dash can be used to sum up or comment on what has gone before in an emphatic way, as in: 'You did not pay within the specified time so we stopped your account – as is normal practice.'
- One dash can also be used like a colon, to indicate two sides of the same theme, but with more emphasis. So you could say either:

  – There can be only one outcome: large-scale redundancies.

  or

  – There can be only one outcome – large-scale redundancies.

  The dash in the second version makes the second part of the sentence stand out more, and therefore makes it starker.

Apostrophes

The apostrophe has three uses.

- It is used to show that a letter or letters have been left out of a word, as in 'don't' for 'do not' or 'let's' for 'let us'. In most business correspondence you should not be using such contractions, however, so this use should not concern you.
- It is often used when writing the plural of a letter, as in 'We must ensure that all the i's are dotted and the t's crossed.'
- Its most common use in a business context is to denote the possessive form of a noun, as in 'Peter's letter' or 'the 'clients' files'. Note that when it is used to denote the possessive of a plural noun that ends in 's', the apostrophe comes after the 's'; with a singular noun or a plural noun that does not end in 's', it comes before the 's'. So you should write 'the customer's account' but 'the customers' accounts', 'ladies' clothing', but 'women's clothing'.

  There is a tendency sometimes to leave the apostrophe out when writing the possessive, particularly in posters or signs. So you will often see 'Ladies Wear' or 'Mens Hairdresser'. Do not be tempted to follow suit. It looks careless or ignorant, and it can affect the clarity of your document.

  Some people have trouble with possessives of names that end in 's' . Should they, for example, write 'Mr Jones's order' or 'Mr Jones' order'? There is no hard and fast rule, and either is acceptable.

Two words that constantly cause problems are 'its' and 'it's' – when should you use the apostrophe and when not? The answer is that it's is short for 'it is', and 'its' means 'belonging to it'.

Quotation Marks

Often called inverted commas, as their name implies these marks indicate quotations. They are used:

- for direct speech, as in: 'He said, "I cannot agree with your proposal."' You will seldom use direct speech in business documents.

- when quoting the exact words of a person, document or publication: 'Norman Tipton wrote of a "potentially damaging recession looming".' In this usage, if the quotation is a complete sentence, then the full stop goes before the quotation mark; if it is just a phrase, but comes at the end of your own sentence, then the full stop comes after the quotation mark.

- for irony, as in 'The Committee has come up with a "radical" new proposal.' The implication is that you do not believe the proposal is actually very radical.

- To indicate a claim or point made by someone else, which you do not want to form part of your own argument, as in 'Smiths have developed a new "quick-dry" paint.' This means that Smiths are claiming that it is quick to dry. You are neither confirming nor denying the claim; it may be that you do not have enough information to make a judgement or that whether the paint is actually quick to dry or not is not important to your argument, it is the claim that matters.

Whether you use single (') or double (") quotation marks is a matter of personal preference. However, very occasionally you may need to write a 'quote within a quote'. Then, if you are using single quotation marks the 'quote within a quote' should be in double marks and vice versa. So you could write:

- Kendall says, 'The provision of unnecessary "executive" gimmicks for management is proving costly.'

or

- Kendall says, "The provision of unnecessary 'executive' gimmicks for management is proving costly."

Exclamation Marks

Exclamation marks, as their name indicates, are used for exclamations. They are seldom necessary or advisable in business correspondence, as you should not be exclaiming, but reasoning and persuading. Some people use them for emphasis, but this is incorrect and looks amateurish. So do not be tempted to write something like 'We offer the cheapest prices in town!' You should be able to provide all the emphasis you need by your choice of words, or with other devices.

There is one situation in which it might be legitimate to use an exclamation mark in less formal business correspondence, and that is in a semi-humorous context to denote irony, as in: 'He claimed he was late because he fell over getting out of bed and hurt his leg!' The implication is 'What a silly excuse.'

Question Marks

There is only one rule for using question marks: they end sentences that are questions, as in: 'Could we meet on Tuesday to discuss your report in detail?' However, you can also use them in informal documents, especially internal memos and e-mails, as a sort of shorthand. So you might write: 'We must meet (? Friday) to discuss the arrangements.' This means 'We must meet to discuss the arrangements. Would Friday suit you?' I must emphasise, however, that it is an informal device, and should only be used in internal and informal communications.

Hyphens

The hyphen is a very useful device, particularly in avoiding confusing or awkward constructions. It is used in the following ways.

- It connects two or more words to form a compound word. This can be a compound noun, as in 'car-park', or a compound adjective, as in 'a ground-floor office'. With compound nouns, it is not always easy to know whether they should be written as one word, hyphenated, or as two words, so you may need to consult your dictionary to be sure (and with some it can be a matter of personal style). With compound adjectives it is simpler. It is usually easier to understand a sentence if compound adjectives are hyphenated. So you would write 'a like-minded colleague' or 'a cost-saving exercise'. However, if the first word is an adverb ending in '-ly', then you should not hyphenate it. So you would write 'a well-designed product', but 'a beautifully designed product'.

- It also connects a letter to a noun to form a compound, as in 'T-junction' or 'U-turn'.

- It is used to differentiate between words beginning with 're-' that are spelt the same but have different meanings. So 'reform' means 'improve', whereas 're-form' means 'form again', 'recount' means 'tell', but 're-count' means 'count again'.

- In a similar way, it can be used to differentiate between two possible meanings of the same passage. So you could have a 'grey flecked carpet' (a 'grey carpet that is flecked' or a 'grey-flecked carpet' (a carpet with grey flecks).

- It makes a compound number, as in 'twenty-eight'.

- It can be used to avoid the awkward repetition of a letter, as in 'co-operate' or 'anti-inflation'.

EXERCISE 25

Punctuate the following passages.

1. The Managing Director who is abroad at present has asked me to reply to your letter concerning the contract for the new equipment although we agree with the terms in general there are a few points we would like explained

2. Our new catalogue enclosed contains details of all our latest lines in particular you may be interested in the following the Newline desk the updated ergonomically designed Comfort swivel chair and the Locksafe filing system as a regular purchaser you could also save money with our valued customers discount

3. We have five different models each with its own special features and they all come in a choice of finishes so whatever your needs you will find one to suit you

4. The expansion of our business is a long term project and we need an efficient sympathetic management consultant to help us a recent report said any small business hoping to expand will find its chances of success greatly improved by the employment of a consultant to advise it we would I think be foolish to embark on this exercise without outside help

5. We are very concerned about your payment record your payments are invariably two months late at the moment we are awaiting payment of invoices 14325 16754 and 23156 all of which are well overdue

CHAPTER 9
Spelling and vocabulary

The rules of spelling in English are not always easy. There are, moreover, a number of words with similar spellings but very different meanings. All of this can make it difficult to use just the right word, and to spell it correctly, every time. You should therefore have a good dictionary handy and *always* refer to it if you are unsure about a word's spelling, or about its precise meaning and usage. If it is only the spelling you are concerned about, there are some excellent little spelling dictionaries available.

No book can hope to cover every word that is likely to cause difficulty; different words cause problems for different people. This chapter will therefore only cover the words that are most commonly used or spelt incorrectly. If there are others with which you regularly have difficulty, then it is a good idea to make a list so that you can refer to it every time you want to use one of them. You will soon learn the correct spelling.

Commonly Misspelt Words

The following points cover the most common spelling errors in business correspondence.

Prefixes

When prefixes like 'dis-', 'un-' and 'mis-' are attached to words beginning with the same letter as the prefix ending, the letter is doubled. So you have:

- dissolve, not disolve
- unnatural, not unatural
- misspell, not mispell

American spellings

If you work for an American company, or all of your business correspondence is with the USA, then you may need to use American spellings. However, some people seem to prefer American spellings, even when they are corresponding with people in the UK or Europe, as though that somehow enhances their image as go-ahead business people. But American spellings are not generally accepted in Britain, and if you use them you will not appear go-ahead, you will appear either careless or ignorant. So use:

- colour, not color
- favourite, not favorite
- centre, not center
- travelled, not traveled
- licence, not license (as a noun – see below)

- all right, not alright
- programme, not program, except a computer program, which is spelt the American way, even in British English

---

Two Nations Divided by a Common Language

Not only are American spellings sometimes different from British; in some cases the whole word may be different. Here are some examples.

- What we call petrol, they call gas.
- What we call the toilet, they call the bathroom.
- What we call a flat they call an apartment (a flat to them is a puncture).
- What we call a holiday, they call a vacation.
- What we call a lift, they call an elevator.
- What we call a lorry, they call a truck.
- What we call a chairman, they call a president.
- What we call a managing director, they call a CEO (chief executive officer).
- What we call a director, they call a vice-president.
- What we call a manager, they call a director.

The final 'l'

As you can see from the above, British English forms the past tense of 'travel' by doubling the 'l', whereas American English does not. The rule for forming both the '-ed' and the '-ing' forms of verbs ending in 'l' (and nouns derived from them) is that you double the 'l' if there is only one vowel before it, and not if there are two. So you would write 'traveller', 'appalling', 'controlled', but 'dealer', 'appealing', 'pooled'.

Adverbs

Adverbs formed from adjectives usually just add '-ly' to the adjective, as in 'quickly', 'recently' and 'slowly'. If the adjective ends in '-ic', however, the adverb is formed by adding '-ally'. So you would write:

- basically, not basicly
- telephonically, not telephonicly
- idiomatically, not idiomaticly

There is just one exception to this rule: 'public' becomes 'publicly', not 'publically'.

'C' and 's'

There are some words that are spelt slightly differently, depending on whether they are used as verbs or nouns. Be sure that you know the difference. They are:

- licence (noun)

  license (verb)

- practice (noun)

  practise (verb)

- advice (noun)

  advise (verb)

If you have difficulty remembering which spelling to use for each form, think of 'advise'. Here the pronunciation changes as well, so you can hear as soon as you use the two forms which is which.

'Dependant' and 'dependent'

Do not confuse these two. 'Dependant' is a noun, and 'dependent' an adjective. So a dependant is someone who is dependent on someone else.

EXERCISE 26

Here is a list of other words with which people often have problems. Some of them are spelt incorrectly here, but not all. Using your dictionary if necessary, identify and correct the errors.

- accumulate

- aquire

- accross

- apreciate

- choatic

- commemmorate

- commission

- concede

- concievable

- conscientious

- defered

- definite

- eighth

- embarass

- exagerate

- fascinate

- feasable

- imminent

- installment

- issueing

- liaison
- manouvre
- occasion
- paralel
- questionaire
- schedule
- sieze
- successful
- supercede
- tarriff
- thorough
- unmistakeable
- writting
- written

Commonly Confused Words

Confusion often arises between words that sound similar but are spelt slightly differently, and between words that have slightly different shades of meaning. This section is not intended to provide a comprehensive list of these words, only to point out those that cause the most confusion.

'Anti-' and 'ante-'

There is often confusion between these prefixes. 'Anti-' means 'against', while 'ante-' means 'before'. So:

- 'antisocial' means 'against society'
- 'anticlimax' means 'against a climax' (i.e. the opposite of a climax)
- 'antedate' means 'date before' something
- 'antecedent' means 'going before'

'For-' and 'fore-'

Similar confusion arises with these prefixes. 'For-' means 'not' or 'against', while 'fore-' means 'before'. So:

- 'forbid' means 'bid not to'
- 'forswear' means 'swear not to'
- 'forgoing' means 'going not' (i.e. going without)
- 'forerunner' means 'something or someone who runs before'

- 'foretell' means 'tell before' (i.e. tell before it happens)
- 'foregoing' means 'going before'

'Infer' and 'imply'

A common mistake is to use 'infer' when you mean 'imply'. 'Imply' means to hint at something, as in: 'He implied that his company would be receptive to an approach from us.' 'Infer' means to gain an impression or draw a conclusion, as in: 'I inferred from what he said that his company would be receptive to an approach from us.' So you could say that you infer what someone else has implied.

'Affect' and 'effect'

These two words can be particularly confusing. 'Affect' is a verb, as in 'The fall in productivity will affect on our profitability.' 'Effect' is the noun derived from 'affect', as in: 'The fall in productivity will have an effect on our productivity.'

However, confusion arises because 'effect' can also be a verb, meaning 'bring about'. So if you were to say, 'The fall in productivity will effect our profitability' you would be saying that the fall will *bring about* your profitability, which is not the same thing at all!

Similar words with different meanings

The following are the most commonly confused pairs of words, with their different meanings.

- **alternate** (every second one): I can work alternate Saturdays.
  alternative (one of two possible options): An alternative strategy would be ...
- **biannual** (twice a year)
  biennial (every two years)
- **complement** (go well with or complete): This line of business would complement our present activities.
  compliment (praise): I must compliment you on an excellent report.
- **continual** (frequent and repeated): We must try to avoid these continual absences.
  continuous (without stop): We hope to achieve continuous production by next month.
- **definite** (not vague): We need a definite answer by tomorrow.
  definitive (final or authoritative): This is the definitive version of the production manual.
- **disinterested** (with no vested interest): If there is any dispute I suggest that we appeal to a disinterested party to resolve it.
  uninterested (not interested): The Chairman is totally uninterested in the day-to-day running of the Company.
- **enquiry** (question): Thank you for your enquiry about our service.
  inquiry (investigation): I have asked the Distribution Manager to conduct a full inquiry into the reasons for the delay.
- **ensure** (make sure): I would be grateful if you could ensure that we are credited with the full amount.
  insure (take out insurance): I trust that the goods are insured against damage in transit.

- **meter** (something that measures): I understand that the error arose as a result of a faulty meter.
  metre (a unit of measurement): The fabric comes in metre lengths.

- **practical** (concerned with practice, not theory): At this stage we should be looking at practical steps to implement the policy.
  practicable (able to be put into practice): The programme you have outlined is hardly practicable in the time allowed.

- **precede** (go before): The decision to close the depot preceded the announcement of the year's profits.
  proceed (begin or go ahead): We shall proceed with the new arrangements as soon as we have your agreement.

- **principal** (main): My principal objection to your proposal is the cost involved.

  principle (fundamental belief or truth): The principles of efficient business practice are the same, whether one is dealing with a one-person business or a multinational corporation.

- **stationary** (standing still): Our van was stationary when your lorry hit it.
  stationery (writing materials): I would like to order the following items of stationery: ...

If you can differentiate between these words in your writing, then you will avoid most of the confusion that commonly arises in business communication. But remember that these lists are not exhaustive. Make friends with your dictionary, and consult it whenever you have any doubts at all.

Answers to Exercises

Exercise 1

There is obviously no single way of making such a summary, but this is an example of what you might have written.

Dear Mr Charles

Thank you for you telephone call this afternoon. I am delighted to hear that you are thinking of visiting our town. As requested, I am writing to confirm the information I gave you over the telephone.

We have a very good theatre, which usually has variety shows in summer and plays in winter. There is also a good museum and the church is famous for its carvings. Moreover, just outside town there is a medieval castle. Your children may be less interested in the museum and the church than you are, but the castle is said to be haunted, so that might appeal to the whole family.

The town also has an excellent, free play park, with a water feature which is always popular with children. And within fairly easy driving distance there are two theme parks, for which you would obviously have to pay. We also have very good sandy beaches nearby – as I said, the nearest is about ten minutes' drive away.

The countryside around here is beautiful, so if you like walking you will find some lovely paths through the woods, and also along the coast. The woodland paths are fairly easy, but there is a lot of climbing and descending along this stretch of the Coast Path.

I enclose a selection of brochures about the area, but if you need any more assistance please do not hesitate to contact me.

Yours sincerely

John Smith
Publicity Officer

Exercise 2

1. 'Fantastic' in line 1 is slang and has no precise meaning. It should be replaced with a more precise word, such as 'useful'.
2. The second and third sentences are irrelevant to a business document.
3. 'Reckons' is slang. 'Believes' would be better.
4. 'Clean up' is slang, and also an exaggeration. 'Significantly increase our turnover' would be better.
5. 'Tricky' is slang, as is 'guy'.
6. 'Persuasive' is a personal opinion, and should not appear in a business document.
7. 'I stuck to my guns' is a colloquialism, and although it might possibly be acceptable in an oral report, it is inappropriate in a written one. Moreover, it is not really relevant to the information you are trying to convey, which is that you believe the other company will agree to equal shares.

8. 'A really good deal' is rather vague, and is based on opinion rather than objective information.
9. 'Blowing my own trumpet' is slang. Moreover, this whole sentence exaggerates your chances of success when there is still so much work to do, and you should certainly not be telling the Board that you are confident of getting your proposal through before they have even considered it!

Exercise 3

If he had borne in mind his purpose and the outcome he wanted to achieve, Donald would probably have written a letter something like this.

Dear Mrs Brown

I was very sorry to see from your letter of 3 December that the legs of one of the occasional tables supplied to you recently are coming off.

I have undertaken a thorough investigation of the problem, and I have discovered what went wrong. I will not bore you with the details; suffice it to say that a combination of human error and problems with our quality control procedures resulted in a few faulty tables leaving our factory. As a result of your letter we have changed our procedures to make sure that this sort of mistake is not made again. We will, of course, be happy to replace any of your tables which are not up to our usual high standards. You only mention one in your letter, but to be on the safe side, I would like to have the whole consignment checked. Could you let me know when it would be convenient for our representative to call? He can then check all your tables and arrange for any that are faulty to be replaced.

Thank you for drawing this problem to my attention, and please accept my apologies for the inconvenience you have been caused.

Yours sincerely

Donald Benson
Production Manager

Of course you would not write it exactly like this because everyone has their own personal style, but the above example has the main ingredients: it is suitable for the purpose in that it keeps the explanation to a minimum but offers an apology; and it is likely to achieve what Donald wants – making Mrs Brown feel good about the company and continuing to buy from them – by not only offering to replace all faulty tables but also sending a representative round to check them.

Exercise 4

Examples 1 and 3 are obviously too full of jargon for members of the public, who would not know what dues are, nor a pre-production costings and proposal form, and would probably not be too sure of the difference between a new edition and a reprint. So 2 would be best for them. Booksellers would know something about the business, and be likely to understand 'dues' and 'out of print', 'reprint' and 'new edition'. But they would probably not know the intricacies of the pre-production costings and proposal form. So they should receive version 3. The first version would, of course, make perfect sense to your colleagues.

Exercise 5

Many of the words used indicate that the letter is aimed at fairly wealthy, discerning clientele. The following are all words associated with this kind of audience.

- original
- elegance
- stylish
- decor

The reference to the company's 'studios' is also intended to create an impression of exclusivity.

How you change it will depend on the alternative clientele at which you wanted to aim the letter. But if, for example, you were writing for a 'middle-of-the-road' audience, you might avoid these 'exclusive' terms, and instead use words such as 'attractive', 'popular' and 'colour scheme' and perhaps refer to the reasonable prices.

Exercise 6

Satish Chaudri has obviously not planned his memo properly – he is just writing down or dictating thoughts as they come to him, and it comes across as chatty, but also woolly and muddled. It is not clear what kind of report he wants from his department managers – does he want them to tell him how much of a problem staff breaks are in their departments, what they think the unions would say, how their staff would react, whether they agree with the principle of keeping a check on the amount of work their staff do – or all of these? At two points he asks them for their opinion, but the main aim of the memo seems to be to obtain information. He also gives no timescale for the production of the reports.

Here is how he might have written his memo to make his aim clearer. He has assembled his information and thought about exactly what he wants from his managers.

From: Satish Chaudri, Managing Director
To: All department managers
Date: 3 April 20XX

WORK BREAKS

It has been observed that some staff appear to be away from their desks rather more than is necessary, although no objective assessment has been made of the extent of the problem. We are therefore considering changes to our working practices, so that staff are required to ask permission before taking a break (apart, of course, from the usual lunch hour). In order that the Board can make a considered decision on this possibly controversial change, I would appreciate it if you could each give me a report before the Board meeting on 20 May, outlining the following:

- whether you feel there is a problem with staff taking excessive breaks in your department, and if so, roughly how many hours you believe are lost as a result

- whether requiring staff to ask permission to leave their desks would address the problem and result in greater productivity or simply lead to time-wasting at their desks rather than away from them

- how staff and unions would react to the introduction of such a system

Exercise 7

1. This would probably best be done by using the same order as the letter; particularly when speaking, it can be easy to miss something out, but if you go through the letter point by point you will know that you have covered everything.
2. The best way to handle this would be by building up an argument, so that you can persuade your audience of the best way forward.
3. Here you need to make an impact immediately, so that the recipient is encouraged to read on. So descending order would be best, with the main point first.
4. On the other hand, you may want to build up to the main point in this case, taking the customer through the various possible options before getting to the price. It is unlikely that you would use the same order as the letter to which you are replying, as you would probably be adding further information to what was actually requested.
5. This would probably be best presented in chronological order, so that it is clear what will be happening when.

Exercise 8

There is obviously no one way in which to reply to such a request – we all have our own style. However, your salutation should reflect the fact that you do not know Mr Kumar, and you should open with a sentence or two about the subject of the letter, which sets the tone for the rest without resorting to clichés. The main body should flow logically; my suggestion would be in descending order of importance, so that you give the good news – that you are prepared to make a donation – first. Then you need an ending that indicates any action to be taken and perhaps a summary. The following example contains all these elements.

Mr Ashok Kumar
Clearwater Youth Club
5 Black Lane
Newtown
NT3 5UV

Dear Mr Kumar

My colleagues and I have considered your request for a contribution towards the costs of running your youth club. As a company, we are keen to help local community projects, and from what you say, your work would appear to be extremely worthwhile. We would therefore be happy to consider making a donation.

However, our policy is only to give money for specific projects, and your letter does not explain what you would want to use any funds we donate for. Because of the nature of our business, we have a particular interest in developing in our young people an appreciation of the outdoors, so if you run any outdoor activities, we feel it would be most appropriate for us to help you with them – either in the form of equipment or in funding trips.

The amount of any donation will depend on what you want to spend it on and the total cost. It would therefore be helpful if you could let me have a list of possible equipment or projects, given the nature of our interests as explained above, together with an approximate cost. We will then consider your request further and decide on the extent to which we can contribute to your work.

I am sure that we will be able to help you, and I look forward to hearing from you with more details in due course.

Yours sincerely

Mark Childs

Marketing Manager

Exercise 9

Use the following checklist to see whether you have included all the elements you should:

- Is your report long enough to need a summary? Is your summary short enough to be read quickly and easily?
- Have you included an introduction? Does it contain only the background to your report?
- Does the body of your report flow logically from one point to the next?
- Have you included a section on the highlights or main points you want to bring to the Chief Executive's attention?
- Does your report need an acknowledgements section and appendices?

Exercise 10

The best formats would be as follows:

1. Table
2. Pie chart
3. Bar chart
4. Graph

Exercise 11

1. 'Thanking' has no subject. It should be: 'Thank you for your help in this matter', since 'Thank you' does not need a subject.
2. There are two unconnected ideas in one sentence. It should be: 'Please call us for a quote. We offer a wide range of other services as well.'

3. 'Including' is a hanging participle. It should be: 'Our latest catalogue, including a range of special offers, is being printed and will be sent to you shortly.'
4. There are too many subsidiary clauses before the subject. It should be something like: 'I have received Mrs Brown's letter complaining about the delay in despatching her order, which you passed on to me. Having conducted a thorough investigation, I am now in a position to report on what went wrong.'
5. 'Which' is a relative pronoun and therefore cannot begin a sentence. It should be: 'Enclosed is our quote for the work on your house which, as you will see, includes replacing the wooden fascia boards with uPVC.'
6. The phrases in the list are part of the same sentence, and should therefore be in parallel. It should therefore be: 'In order to survive we need to:
   a. raise our profile in the market
   b. increase our productivity
   c. improve our customer service.'
7. The two clauses contain ideas that are close enough to be included in the same sentence, but they should be separated by a conjunction or a semicolon. The best way of expressing it would be: 'I am aware of all the hard work you have put in on behalf of the company, and I will consider your request carefully.'
8. There are too many unconnected ideas in one sentence. It should be: 'There appears to have been some misunderstanding regarding my reservation. I requested a room only, and just for one night, whereas your confirmation is for two nights' bed and breakfast. I would be grateful if you could amend your records.'

Exercise 12

As I have said, there is no precise rule about where to start a new paragraph, but the letter should look something like this:

Dear Mr Iqbal

Following our conversation last week, I would like to confirm the arrangements for your sales conference on 15 and 16 May.

We have reserved the small conference room for you. This seats 40 people, and since there will only be 30 attending there will be plenty of room for everyone. We will provide seating and tables in a horseshoe layout, as you requested. We will also provide a flip chart and easel and an overhead projector. If you also need a digital projector, one can be made available; you need only ask me on the day.

We will serve coffee and tea at 11 a.m. and 3.30 p.m. and lunch at 1 p.m. on both days, in a separate room. Lunch menus are attached. I understand that only the wine with the meal is to be charged to your company, and that any other drinks should be paid for. A private bar will be set aside for your use.

I have also reserved 15 rooms with private baths for those who are staying overnight.

I look forward to seeing you on the 15th, and thank you for choosing our hotel for your venue.

Yours sincerely

Keith Blackstone
Conference Manager

Exercise 13

Use the following checklist to see whether you have included everything you should.

- Are all your topic sentences either the first or the second sentences in their paragraphs?
- Do they all indicate what the paragraph is going to be about?
- Does each paragraph flow naturally from the one before it?
- Do your linking devices indicate to the reader how the paragraph is going to link with what has gone before?

Exercise 14

The letter is very formal, cold and unfriendly because:

- Catherine Porter addresses Mrs Maxwell as 'Dear Madam'.
- She hides behind the impersonal 'we' rather than using the personal (and therefore more friendly) 'I'.
- She starts her letter with the formal 'We are in receipt of your letter' rather than one of the friendlier openings suggested in Chapter 3.
- She says 'Your account has been credited' (passive voice), which is impersonal, rather than the active and therefore more direct and friendly 'I have credited your account.'
- Although she acknowledges that her company made an error, she makes no apology.
- She rejects Mrs Maxwell's request for compensation very abruptly. She could be more tactful, while still sticking to the company's policy.

This is how the letter might have been written to make it more conversational in style, and friendlier.

CARSTAIRS CLOTHING COMPANY
43 Gorton Road, Marsby, MB2 4HY
Tel. 01921 143267

26 August 20XX

Mrs A. Maxwell
13 Thrixton Crescent
Charterborough
LT14 6TU

Dear Mrs Maxwell

I was very sorry to see from your letter of 15 August that you are still being charged for the dress you returned to us. I have investigated the matter, and it appears that we did indeed receive it, but that owing to an error in the Accounts Department, your account was not adjusted. I do apologise for this oversight, and for the inconvenience you have been caused. I have now credited your account.

▶

I am afraid, however, that I cannot give you any financial compensation. We are always happy to consider claims for compensation when there has been financial loss as a result of our error, but as I understand it, you have not suffered any loss.

I am sorry you have had to write to us about this matter, and I hope you understand our position on the question of compensation.

Yours sincerely

Catherine Porter
Customer Relations Manager

Exercise 15

These are the main problems with the letter.

- 'Taken on board' is jargon, designed to sound impressive. 'Considered' would be simpler.
- 'Conducted a thorough investigation ... leaving no stone unturned and looking at all the policies on offer' is tautology. Conducting a thorough investigation involves looking at all the policies (and leaving no stone unturned – see below).
- 'Leaving no stone unturned' is a cliché.
- 'Downside' is jargon. 'Disadvantage' is more direct (and more correct, since 'downside' has not yet found its way into most standard dictionaries).
- 'In the event that' is 'commercialese'. It means simply 'if'.
- 'Utilise' is another example of jargon used to make the letter sound impressive. What is wrong with 'use'?
- 'At your earliest convenience' is another example of old-fashioned 'commercialese'. It means simply 'as soon as possible'.
- 'Provision can be made' means 'can be provided' – it is an example of an unnecessary abstract noun and sounds convoluted.

Exercise 16

This is the sort of memo you might have written (depending on your particular organisation and the course you have chosen to write about).

To:
From:
Date:

Our organisation prides itself on encouraging its staff to undertake continuous professional development - a policy which I believe contributes to our success.

I have received information about a course on health and safety in the workplace, which I feel would be extremely useful, not only in my current role but also in the future if, as I hope to do, I progress through the company. The knowledge I acquire will also be of great benefit to the organisation, and I envisage being able to provide feedback to my colleagues. The course is certificated, with an assessment element included.

I enclose a leaflet about the course for your information. As you will see, it lasts for a full week and is residential. I would therefore appreciate it if you could agree to my taking that week off to attend. The fee for the week is £1,500, and I would also be grateful if the organisation could meet that cost.

I look forward to hearing from you.

This fulfils the criteria of being friendly and courteous without being sycophantic, and of building up to the request.

Exercise 17

This is the kind of response you might have written.

To:
From:
Date:

I have considered your request to attend the health and safety course whose details you sent me. It does seem to be a good course, and for that reason, I have given careful thought to your request, as well as discussing its potential benefits for our organisation with different people.

As you say, our policy is to encourage the personal and professional development of our employees. However, we obviously also have to consider what the organisation will get out of a course such as this, especially if we are to release a key member of staff for a week. We also have to take into account the fact that we already have several people on our staff who have just the kind of expertise this course appears to offer. I am afraid, therefore, that I have come to the conclusion that there are likely to be few additional advantages to the organisation as a whole in your attending, and that I could not justify the expenditure.

I am sorry to disappoint you, and I do not want to put you off taking advantage of training opportunities that arise. So if you come across any other courses that are more directly related to our specific priorities, please do approach me again.

Exercise 18

Use the following checklist to see whether your letter is likely to be effective.

- Is it clearly aimed at a particular audience?
- Does it make the benefits your organisation can offer your audience clear?
- Does it conform to the AIDA or four Ps formula, or both?
- Have you identified a USP or emotional buying trigger? Is it important enough to be emphasised, or have you included it just for the sake of it? (Remember that these are devices to be used *if* they apply to your situation; they are not essential to your letter.)

Exercise 19

This is the kind of memo you might have written. However, if yours is very different, it does not mean that it is wrong – simply that your meeting will be different from the one outlined here. As long as your memo or e-mail makes it clear when and where the meeting will be held, and your agenda is clear and decision driven (and covers everything you think needs to be discussed), then it will serve its purpose.

To: (List the people in your organisation who might be involved)
From:
Date:

Meeting re the staff Christmas party

I have been asked to arrange a meeting to discuss arrangements for this year's party. The meeting will be held in Room 217 at 2 p.m. on Thursday, 10 October. The agenda is set out below. Please could you let me know if you cannot attend. Thank you.

AGENDA

1. To receive apologies for absence
2. To agree the date of the staff Christmas party
3. To decide the format for the evening
   (a) Should dinner be provided?
   (b) Should there be a theme?
   (c) Should there be dancing?
4. To consider possible venues
5. To allocate responsibilities for follow-up action
   (a) Contacting potential venues and obtaining prices, including dinner if it is to be included
   (b) Arranging for a band or disco if there is to be dancing
   (c) Approaching Management to establish whether the organisation will subsidise the event
6. To agree the date of the next meeting

Exercise 20

Since the minutes you write will depend on what is said at the meeting, it is impossible even to provide an example of what you might have written. So compare your minutes with the example shown in the text to see whether they follow a similar format.

Exercise 21

Your notes should include the following:

- your order number
- details of your good relationship with the supplier in the past (assuming it was good – if it was not, then perhaps you should have switched to another supplier before now!)
- details of how the delivery differed from your order

- the catalogue number of the style of furniture you ordered
- if you know it, the catalogue number of the 12 sets that were the wrong style
- perhaps an indication of the inconvenience that has been caused by the problem
- a request that these 12 be replaced (with the supplier collecting them), and that the order be filled in full
- throughout, a note of words that you might want to remember to use in order to make your call friendly, but still get your point across

Exercise 22

This is the kind of letter you might write:

Dear Mr Smith

I was very sorry to hear from your telephone call on Tuesday that we got your order so wrong. Please accept my apologies for the inconvenience our error has caused you.

I have investigated the problem, and it appears that our order-processing department confused your order with that of another customer, with the result that half of your order went to them, and half of theirs came to you. We are in the process of taking remedial action.

I have arranged for 14 sets of workstations and chairs of the correct style (number 103 in our catalogue) to be delivered to you tomorrow, and for the 12 sets that are the wrong style (number 124 in the catalogue) to be collected at the same time.

To compensate you for the inconvenience you have suffered as a result of the delay, I am arranging for the original invoice (for 28 sets) to stand, instead of issuing a new invoice for the full order.

I hope this meets with your approval, and apologise, once again, for our error.

Yours sincerely

Peter Jones
Marketing Manager

Exercise 23

Use the following checklist to ensure that your report is clearly and logically argued, and that you have considered all aspects of the matter.

- Have you included all the information that is relevant to the point you want to make (including information that might not have been included in the original report and information that might not support your conclusion)?
- Have you presented it in a logical order?
- Have you included your own opinions? If so, is it clear that they are opinions, not facts?

- Have you looked at all sides of the issue before coming to your conclusion?
- Have you thought of any counter-arguments (such as the reasons for the department or organisation not having adopted your suggested changes already)?
- Have you refuted those arguments with reference to the information provided in the main body of the report?

Exercise 24

1. The Board was asked to consider the proposal carefully. It was given conditional approval only after a lengthy discussion.
2. On Wednesday, Keith Hamilton had a meeting with Simon Kitson. Keith said that the following week he would be in Paris, where the company has its European office, so he could discuss the contract then.
3. We have had a good response to our advertisement for a sales manager, and Emma Johnson would like to discuss the applications with you and me on Tuesday.
4. I do not mind you asking for time off, but it would be nice to see you occasionally working late as well. You appear to be getting rather behind with your work, which is affecting the efficiency of the whole department.
5. You say that you have not seen the delivery note and the invoice. Your accountant and I have had a long discussion about this, and I think you will find that he has copies.
6. The Committee has decided that every member, together with his or her partner, has the right to use the facilities of the centre.
7. Having considered all the estimates, I believe we should accept either Axis's or Mainland Distribution's. None of the other firms was able to match their prices or delivery times.
8. Please can you see to it that every secretary and clerk, including the directors' PAs, is made aware of the new house style. We must ensure that we create not only a good image but also a consistent one.
9. We can offer a choice of three conference rooms, any of which would suit your requirements. We will serve lunch at 12.30 p.m. as requested.
10. I am afraid that I differ with you over the best way forward for the development. Looking at the two plans, I think the layout of the second is much more flexible.

Exercise 25

Because punctuation is to a certain extent a matter of personal taste, there are different ways of punctuating any passage. However, these are the suggested answers.

1. The Managing Director, who is abroad at present, has asked me to reply to your letter concerning the contract for the new equipment. Although we agree with the terms in general, there are a few points we would like explained.

2. Our new catalogue (enclosed) contains details of all our latest lines. In particular you may be interested in the following: the Newline desk; the updated, ergonomically designed Comfort swivel chair; and the Locksafe filing system. As a regular purchaser you could also save money with our valued customers' discount.

3. We have five different models – each with its own special features – and they all come in a choice of finishes. So whatever your needs you will find one to suit you.

4. The expansion of our business is a long-term project and we need an efficient, sympathetic management consultant to help us. A recent report said, 'Any small business hoping to expand will find its chances of success greatly improved by the employment of a consultant to advise it.' We would, I think, be foolish to embark on this exercise without outside help.

5. We are very concerned about your payment record; your payments are invariably two months late. At the moment we are awaiting payment of invoices 14325, 16754 and 23156, all of which are well overdue.

Exercise 26

Here is the list again with the incorrect words identified and corrected.

- accumulate
- (X) acquire
- (X) across
- (X) appreciate
- (X) chaotic
- (X) commemorate
- commission
- concede
- (X) conceivable
- conscientious
- (X) deferred
- definite
- eighth
- (X) embarrass
- (X) exaggerate
- fascinate
- (X) feasible
- imminent
- (X) instalment
- (X) issuing
- liaison
- (X) manoeuvre

- occasion
- (X) parallel
- (X) questionnaire
- schedule
- (X) seize
- successful
- (X) supersede
- (X) tariff
- thorough
- (X) unmistakable
- (X) writing
- written

Further reading

Your first priority should be a good dictionary. The best are published by Oxford University Press, Collins, Chambers and Longman. They come in a variety of sizes, from pocket editions to large two-volume tomes. Choose one that suits your needs and budget.

Other books you might like to refer to are:

Improve Your Punctuation and Grammar, Marion Field (How To Books, 2009)

Improve Your Written English, Marion Field (How To Books, 2009). A good general guide to writing.

New Oxford Dictionary for Writers and Editors (Oxford University Press, 2005). An invaluable guide, based on OUP's house style, which shows you how to spell unusual or difficult words, when to hyphenate words and a great deal more.

Pocket Fowler's Modern English Usage, Edited by Robert Allen (Oxford University Press, 2004). The 'bible' of English usage.

Roget's Thesaurus of English Words and Phrases, Edited by George Davidson (Penguin, 2004). The classic guide to synonyms and antonyms – ideal for those occasions when you cannot think of the precise word you need.

Spell Well, Marion Field (How To Books, 2005).

Troublesome Words, Bill Bryson (Penguin, 2002). A very good guide to words that give problems.

Glossary

Adjective. A word that qualifies a noun, e.g. little, brown, round.

Adverb. A word that qualifies a verb, adjective, preposition or other adverb, e.g. well, clearly, very.

AIDA. A formula for remembering the order in which an advertisement or sales letter should be written. Stands for Attention, Interest, Desire, Action.

Ampersand. The symbol &. An abbreviation for 'and'.

Appendix. A section of a report or book that usually gives full details of matters not discussed in detail in the main part.

Bar chart. A method of presenting figures visually. Particularly useful for comparing two or more sets of figures at a particular time.

bcc. Typed only on copies of a document to indicate that a copy is being sent to the person named – a 'blind copy'. Used instead of 'cc' when you do not want the document's addressee to know that you are sending a copy to a third party.

cc. Typed on a document to indicate that a copy is being sent to the person named.

Charting. A method of writing an outline for a document, involving making a chart of ideas you want to express.

Circumlocution. A phrase or clause that uses more words than are necessary to express an idea.

Clause. A group of words within a sentence that has a subject and a predicate.

Cliché. An expression that has been used so often that it has become hackneyed.

Colloquialism. An expression that is common in speech but is not acceptable in written English.

Complex sentence. A sentence that contains a main clause and one or more subordinate clauses.

Complimentary close. The ending of a letter. Usually 'Yours sincerely' or 'Yours faithfully' in business correspondence.

Compound sentence. A sentence that contains two or more clauses joined by a co-ordinating conjunction.

Compound complex sentence. A sentence that contains two or more main clauses and one or more subordinate clauses.

Conjunction. A word that links two words, phrases or clauses, e.g. and, but, however.

Co-ordinating conjunction. A conjunction that joins two clauses of equal weight.

Deduction. A method of reasoning from one premise to another to reach a conclusion.

Edit. To check a piece of writing for spelling, grammatical and stylistic errors.

Emotional buying trigger. An appeal to an emotion or instinct in selling or advertising.

Enc. Typed at the bottom of a letter to indicate that something is enclosed.

Four Ps. A formula for remembering how to write a sales letter. Stands for Promise, Picture, Proof, Push.

Freewriting. A method of writing an outline for a document, involving writing freely as ideas occur to you.

Fyi. For your information. Typed on copies of correspondence sent to third parties to indicate that no action is expected from them.

Graph. A method of presenting figures visually. Particularly useful to show a trend over time.

Hanging participle. A participle that introduces an adjectival phrase with no noun to qualify.

Indexing. A method of standardising the presentation of figures so that different fields can be compared. Usually involves giving the figures for Year 1 a value of 100, and relating subsequent years' figures to that.

Induction. A method of reaching a conclusion from one's own experience or observation rather than by reasoning from one premise to another.

Inside address. The name and address of the person to whom you are writing, which appear at the top of a letter.

Jargon. Language that is specific to a particular group or profession.

Listing. A method of writing an outline for a document, involving listing the points you want to make.

Minutes. A formal record of discussions and decisions at a meeting.

Noun. A word that is used to name a person, place or thing, e.g. letter, Harriet Cornish, London.

Object. The person or thing that has the action of the verb done to it. Must be a noun or a pronoun.

Parentheses. Another word for round brackets.

Phrase. A group of words within a sentence that does not have a subject and a predicate.

Pie chart. A method of showing figures visually. Particularly useful for showing the segmentation of a total figure.

pp. Typed or written by a signature, when the signatory is signing a letter on behalf of someone else.

Predicate. The part of a sentence that describes what the subject did or was. Must contain a verb.

Preposition. A word that describes the relationship of one person or thing to another, e.g. by, from, for.

Pronoun. A word used instead of a noun, e.g. she, him, your.

Salutation. The opening of a letter. Usually begins 'Dear ...'

Sentence. A group of words complete in itself. Must contain a subject and a predicate.

Simple sentence. A sentence containing only one clause.

Subject. The person or thing a sentence is about. Must be either a noun or a pronoun.

Subordinate clause. A clause that is dependent on the rest of the sentence for its meaning or relevance.

Subordinating conjunction. A conjunction that joins a subordinate clause to the rest of the sentence.

Tautology. Saying the same thing twice in different words.

Topic sentence. A sentence that indicates the topic of a paragraph.

Unique selling proposition. Something that makes a product or service unique.

Vague qualifier. An imprecise adjective or adverb that adds nothing to the reader's understanding.

Verb. A word that describes what is done by or what happens to the subject of a sentence, e.g. agree, have written, will decide.

Index

Quick Solutions to Common Errors in English

An A-Z guide to spelling, punctuation and grammar

Angela Burt

'You will never doubt your written English again.' – *Evening Standard*

'A straightforward and accessible handbook for anyone who ever has a query about correct English – and that's all of us.' – *Freelance News*

'This is an excellent book; good value and useful… buy it!' – *V. Tilbury, Cranfield University*

ISBN 978-1-84528-361-2

Writing a Report

How to prepare, write and present effective reports

John Bowden

'What is special about the text is that it is more than just how to 'write reports'; it gives that extra really powerful information that can, and often does, make a difference. It is by far the most informative text covering report writing that I have seen… This book would be a valuable resource to any practising manager. ' – *Training Journal*

'With the help of this sensible step-by-step guide, anybody can develop first-rate report writing skills.' – *Building Engineer*

ISBN 978-1-84528-293-6

Model Everyday Letters

How to write and set out formal letters and documents

ANGELA BURT

'…from writing a formal acceptance of a wedding invitation, putting together a job application letter and saying the right thing in an absence note for a child who has been away from school… There are correct and incorrect ways of this kind of everyday writing, and Angela Burt shows just how it should be done.' – Writers' News

'…so helpful in guiding you through the formalities and principles.' – Writing Magazine

ISBN 978-1-84528-316-2

Improve Your Punctuation and Grammar

MARION FIELD

'Invaluable guide…after reading this book, you will never again find yourself using a comma instead of a semi-colon.' – Evening Standard

'I can't recommend this book highly enough. Every writer should have a copy.' – Writers' Bulletin

ISBN 978-1-84528-329-2

Presenting With Power

SHAY McCONNON

'His engaging style of presentation ... captivates his audience whatever their background or current state of motivation.' Director, Walkers Snack Foods

ISBN 978-1-84528-160-1

Getting Your Point Across

PHILLIP KHAN-PANNI

'I've heard Phillip speak on this subject many times and every time I learn something new. Now this book gives me all those good ideas in a format that I can dip into over and over again.' Paul Bridle – Executive Coach and Leadership Consultant.

ISBN 978-1-84528-191-5

TOUCH TYPING IN TEN HOURS

ANN DOBSON

With this book you can learn to 'touch type' in ten hours at a *fraction of the cost* of a course. It will also take you *less time* than the average course and, best of all, *you can learn in your own home or office.* Just think how much time you will save in your working day - and you will be able to concentrate on the content rather than finding the correct letters.

Touch Type in Ten Hours contains easy-to-use lessons divided into manageable one hour blocks, and there are plenty of exercises to consolidate what you have learned. There is also a reference guide giving useful 'tips of the trade'.

ISBN 978-1-84528-340-7

How To Books are available through all good bookshops, or you can order direct from us through Grantham Book Services.

Tel: +44 (0)1476 541080
Fax: +44 (0)1476 541061
Email: orders@gbs.tbs-ltd.co.uk

Or via our website
www.howtobooks.co.uk

To order via any of these methods please quote the title(s) of the book(s) and your credit card number together with its expiry date.

For further information about our books and catalogue, please contact:

How To Books
Spring Hill House
Spring Hill Road
Begbroke
Oxford OX5 1RX

Visit our web site at
www.howtobooks.co.uk

Or you can contact us by email at info@howtobooks.co.uk